GETTING STARTED

knitting socks

Ann Budd

INTERWEAVE PRESS

Technical editor, Lori Gayle
Photographs, Joe Coca
Text © 2007, Interweave Press LLC
Illustrations © 2007, Interweave Press LLC
Photography © 2007, Interweave Press LLC

 INTERWEAVE PRESS.
201 East Fourth Street
Loveland, Colorado 80537 USA
interweavebooks.com

Printed in China through Asia Pacific Offset

Library of Congress Cataloging-in-Publication Data

Budd, Ann, 1956–
   Getting started knitting socks / Ann Budd, author.
      p. cm.
   Includes bibliographical references and index.
   ISBN 978-1-59668-029-6 (hardcover)
   1. Knitting—Patterns. 2. Socks. I. Title.
   TT825.B82 2007
   746.43'2041—dc22

                                   2007001884

10 9 8 7 6 5 4 3

acknowledgments

As all books, *Getting Started Knitting Socks* was not an individual effort.

The projects in this book could never have been knitted without the wonderful yarns produced by manufacturers across the country. Louet Sales generously donated all of the yarn for the basic step-by-step photographs, basic sock patterns, and swatches of stitch patterns. Yarns were also provided by Brown Sheep Company, Cascade Yarns, Coats & Clark, Koigu Wool Designs, Unicorn Books & Crafts, Lion Brand, Lorna's Laces, The Wooly West, and Westminster Fibers.

The folks at Interweave Press—particularly Tricia Waddell, Rebecca Campbell, Anne Merrow, and Linda Stark—provided suggestions and collaboration every step of the way. Lori Gayle ensured that the instructions are clear and correct (if there are any errors, I'm to blame). And the book wouldn't be a visual treat without the efforts of Joe Coca, Paulette Livers, Ann Swanson, and Alan Bernhard. To all of you, my sincerest thanks.

I also want to give a nod to my Fun Club friends Jane, Judy, Gail, Maggie, Mary Kay, and Weezie for giving me a break every month, and to my somewhat-weekly knitting pals Ann, Beege, Carmen, Darcy, Heide, Judy, Karen, and Lisa for listening to me go on and on about all aspects of handknitted socks.

Last, but certainly not least, deep thanks to my boys David, Alex, Eric, and Nicholas for patiently waiting for me to finish a row (or round) of knitting before asking me do anything else.

contents

Introduction

1 Materials 8
Yarn 9
Needles 11
Other Tools 13

2 Sock Basics 14
Measuring Gauge 17
Ways to Knit Socks in Rounds 18
Casting On 20
Join for Working in the Round 23
Cuff 24
Leg 25
Heel Flap 26
Heel Turn 28
Gussets 31
Foot 37
Toe 39
Finishing 47

3 Basic Sock Instructions 48
Choosing a Size 49
Basic Pattern for 8 Stitches/Inch 52
Basic Pattern for 7 Stitches/Inch 54
Basic Pattern for 6 Stitches/Inch 56
Basic Pattern for 5 Stitches/Inch 58
Basic Pattern for 4 Stitches/Inch 60

4 Color and Texture the Easy Way 62
PROJECTS
Wide Stripes Socks 64
Narrow Stripes Socks 66
Spiral Stripes Socks 68
Magic Stripes Socks 70
Bouclé Socks 72

5 Adding Your Own
Color and Texture 74

Stripe Patterns 75

PROJECTS

Fibonacci Stripes Socks 76

Magic Ball Socks 80

Rib Patterns 84

PROJECTS

Seeded Rib Socks 88

Spiral Rib Socks 92

Cable Patterns 96

PROJECTS

Right-Twist Cable Rib Socks 100

Cable Clock Socks 104

Lace Patterns 108

PROJECTS

Herringbone Lace Socks 112

Chevron Lace Socks 116

6 Cuff and Leg
Variations 120

PROJECTS

Picot Anklets 122

Ruffle Cuff Anklets 125

Knee Socks 128

Glossary of
Abbreviations and Terms 132

Sources for Supplies 134

Bibliography 135

Index 136

Introduction

I've developed a relationship with handknitted socks that's bordering on a love affair. From the moment I slip on my socks in the morning to the moment I take them off at night, my legs are secretly being hugged, my heels gently cupped, and my feet caressed. While no one is looking, my socks embrace and cushion every step I take. In return they only ask not be put in the dryer. Since I was given my first pair of handknitted socks about ten years ago, I've gradually forsaken all commercially manufactured substitutes. My feet and I are very happy.

So why are so many knitters hesitant to knit socks? Do they see folly in knitting something that no one sees, or worse, something that's bound to wear out? Do they worry that socks are too complicated to knit—all those pointy needles and tricky maneuvers? I suspect that it's a little bit of each. But I also suspect that it's because they haven't experienced the pleasures of hand-knitted socks firsthand. Put on a pair of handknitted socks and any excuse is trivial. I'm now evangelistic in my desire to bring the same pleasure to all knitters (and their friends).

Sure, there are a number of techniques used in sock knitting that don't arise in other projects—double-pointed needles, short-rows, picking up stitches, and the dreaded Kitchener stitch. But, when approached one at a time, none of these techniques is any more difficult than learning the basic knit and purl stitches. If you can knit and purl, you can knit your own socks. Follow the clear steps, photographs, and illustrations in this book and you'll wonder why you waited so long.

Start by gathering the materials listed in Chapter 1, then follow the step-by-step instructions in Chapter 2. Once you've mastered your first pair of socks (and I promise you, it's not hard), you'll eagerly reach for your needles to start another pair. You can choose a variety of sizes and weights of yarn to make dozens of socks following the basic patterns for 4 to 8 stitches to the inch. If you get tired of the basic sock, add some color or texture—ribs, cables, or lace. Adjust the length of the leg or the type of cuff. To get you started, I've provided patterns for sixteen variations—follow the patterns as written or use them as a first step for your own design ideas.

Before you know it, you'll start your own love affair.

1 Materials

Yarn

First and foremost, you'll need some yarn. Choosing yarn can be a lot of fun, but the choices can be overwhelming. You'll want to consider the size or weight of the yarn, the fiber content, and the color.

Yarn Weight

It's a good idea to start by deciding on the weight of sock you want. Do you want a thick, rugged boot sock? A thin, delicate stocking? If you want to wear your handknitted socks in shoes, you'll need to choose lightweight yarn—fingering weight is best, but if your shoes have a loose fit, you can probably use sportweight yarn. Socks worn with loose fitting shoes such as utility boots, clogs, Crocs, Birkenstocks, or Danskos, can be knitted with thicker yarn—perhaps as thick as worsted weight. Save chunky-weight yarns for socks that will be worn alone as slippers.

Socks can be knitted with a variety of yarn weights. Clockwise from far left: Chunky-weight yarn at 4 stitches/inch, worsted-weight yarn at 5 stitches/inch, sportweight yarn at 6 stitches/inch, sportweight yarn at 7 stitches/inch, fingering-weight yarn at 8 stitches/inch.

How Much Yarn Will You Need?

The amount of yarn you need depends on the gauge and sock size. In general, the finer the yarn and the bigger the sock, the more yarn you'll need. If you plan to add a heavily textured pattern such as cables, you'll also need more yarn.

Gauge (stitches/inch)	child M	child L	adult S	adult M	adult L
4	125	170	202	252	296 yards
	115	156	185	231	271 meters
5	138	188	224	279	329 yards
	126	172	205	255	301 meters
6	195	266	317	394	466 yards
	179	243	290	361	426 meters
7	215	293	349	434	513 yards
	197	268	319	397	469 meters
8	236	322	384	477	564 yards
	216	294	351	437	516 meters

Fiber Content

There are dozens of yarns that make great socks, many of which are marketed specifically as "sock yarn." Most commonly, these yarns contain a high percentage of wool due to wool's superior absorbency and warmth. If you worry about wool irritating sensitive skin, consider yarns made from merino wool—merino is exceptionally soft, and many people who may be unable to wear wool next to their skin can wear merino socks. Don't give up on handknitted socks if you find any kind of wool uncomfortable—there are cotton and synthetic yarns that are also good choices. See the Sources for Supplies on page 134 for some of my favorites. Many dedicated sock yarns include a percentage of nylon that helps make the yarn more durable—an important consideration for high-friction areas such as heels and toes. Most knitting shops carry nylon reinforcing thread that can be knitted along with the yarn while working the heels and toes. This reinforcing thread not only prevents holes from forming, it also resists breaking itself. If the yarn does wear away, you'll still have the thread holding the socks together and providing a good foundation for darning.

Color

Here's where you can have loads of fun. Over the past decade, yarn companies have been manufacturing exciting yarns that make knitting socks really interesting. Besides a veritable rainbow of color possibilities, there are yarns created to produce ingenious patterns. I love using these self-patterning yarns because it's so much fun to watch the patterns evolve. And even though I can see the individual colors in the balls of these yarns, I never really know what pattern they'll produce until I knit them up. I'm always surprised.

Needles

You can't knit a pair of socks without knitting needles. Historically, socks have been knitted on double-pointed needles, either in sets of four or five. If you're uncomfortable managing so many needles, you can also knit socks on two circular needles, or even on one very long circular needle. Double-pointed needles come in various lengths, from 5" (12.5 cm) to 10" (25.5 cm); most knitters prefer the shorter lengths (5 to 6" [12.5 to 15 cm]) for socks because there are relatively few stitches on each needle. If you want to avoid all those individual needles, you can work socks on a short circular needle. There are 12" (30 cm) circular needles made just for knitting socks. But because they are so short, some knitters find them difficult to handle. Many knitters prefer to use two circular needles instead, working one-half of the stitches on each needle. You can use any length needle here, but I find that 16" (40 cm) needles work best for me—the tips that aren't being used hang down far enough to be out of the way, but not so far that they tangle with each other or get caught on nearby objects such as chair arms, pillows, or the ball of yarn. Another option is to use one very long circular needle. I prefer working on a 40" (100 cm) needle because the long cable provides lots of flexibility. If you're unfamiliar with any of these ways to knit socks, check out the box on pages 18–19.

No matter what type of needle(s) you choose, you'll also have a choice in materials. The most common needles come in wood, plastic, or metal. Wood needles feel warm in your hands, can get smoother with use, and make for quiet knitting. But they can break, especially the smaller sizes. Plastic needles, which are also quiet, have a little flexibility that can reduce hand and wrist strain. Metal needles are strong and durable and are notorious for producing the familiar "click, clack" associated with knitting.

You can knit socks on a variety of needles made from wood, plastic, or metal: double-pointed, short circular, or long circular.

The needle size will depend on the size of the yarn you choose and the thickness of the fabric you want to produce. The table below gives guidelines for stockinette stitch. Don't feel locked into these numbers. I like thick, sturdy socks, so I typically knit at tighter gauges than recommended here. For example, I like to knit sportweight yarn at a gauge of 7 or 8 stitches per inch (28 or 32 stitches/4" [10 cm]), which is a more typical gauge for fingering-weight yarn.

From lower left to upper right: fingering-weight yarn at 8 stitches/inch, sportweight yarn at 7 stitches/inch, DK-weight yarn at 6 stitches/inch, worsted-weight yarn at 5 stitches/inch, chunky-weight yarn at 4 stitches/inch.

Standard Yarn, Needle Sizes, and Gauges

Yarn Size	Needle Size	Gauge (stitches/4")
#1 Super Fine (fingering)	U.S. 1–3 2.25–3.25 mm	27–32
#2 Fine (sport)	U.S. 3–5 3.25–3.75 mm	23–26
#3 Light (DK)	U.S. 5–7 3.75–4.5 mm	21–24
#4 Medium (worsted)	U.S. 7–9 4.5–5.5 mm	16–20
#5 Bulky (chunky)	U.S. 9–11 5.5–8 mm	12–15

Other Tools

In addition to yarn and needles, there are only a few tools that you'll need. You'll want a tape measure or ruler to measure gauge and leg and foot lengths. You'll also want a pair of small scissors for trimming yarn ends and a tapestry needle to finish off the toe and weave in yarn ends.

Depending on what type of stitch or color pattern you're knitting, you may want ring markers for marking groups of stitches on the needles or open-ring markers for marking key rows; a row counter for keeping track of multi-row stitch patterns; stitch holders for holding stitches that are not actively being knitted (for example, to hold the instep stitches while you work the heel); a cable needle if you're working a cable pattern; reinforcing thread/yarn for heels and toes; a pencil and paper for taking notes (especially if you make a change to the pattern on one sock—you'll want to be sure that the second sock matches); and, if you really want to be traditional, sock blockers for blocking the finished socks.

In addition to a tape measure and ruler, small scissors, and a tapestry needle, you may want stitch holders, open-ring markers, closed-ring markers, a row counter, a cable needle, and reinforcing thread.

2 Sock Basics

In Western countries, socks are typically worked from the leg down to the toe (in many Eastern countries, they're worked in the opposite direction). The size is determined by the circumference of the widest part of the foot. A sock begins with stitches cast on for the leg. The stitches are joined into a circle and worked in the round to the beginning of the heel. The back of the heel, or heel flap, is worked back and forth in rows on half of the total number of stitches. To reinforce the back of the heel, it is commonly worked in a pattern of slipped and knitted stitches that creates a dense fabric. At the end of the heel flap, short-rows are worked to give a cup shape that hugs the heel. This is the part that mystifies many new sock knitters; as if by magic, the odd shape emerges. After the heel is shaped, gusset stitches are picked up along the edges of the heel flap and the entire foot is worked in the round to the toes. The stitches picked up along the sides of the heel flap are reduced as the gusset is worked to taper the foot, forming distinctive diagonal lines of stitches. The foot is worked straight until it measures to about the base of the little toe. Then stitches are decreased along each side of the foot, evenly and consistently, until 8 to 16 stitches remain. Finally, these remaining stitches are grafted together to produce a comfortable, rounded tip.

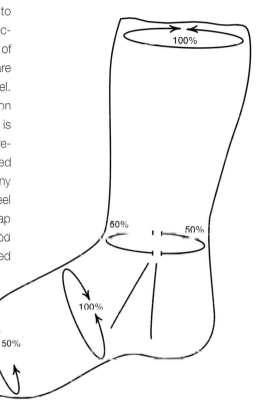

Socks instructions follow a simple formula of percentages—100% of the stitches are worked for the leg, 50% are worked for the heel, 100% are worked for the foot. The toe is decreased gradually to 50%, then rapidly to about 20%.

In general, sock Instructions follow a simple formula based on the foot circumference. Let's say that our circumference is 8" (20.5 cm) and we're working at a gauge of 5 stitches to the inch. Multiplying the gauge by the circumference, we know that we'll need 40 stitches for the foot. Once you know this number, the others fall into place: The same number of stitches (100%) is used for the leg as for the foot (40 stitches). Half of these stitches (50%; 20 stitches) are used to work the heel flap; the other half (20 stitches) form the top of the foot (instep). The heel flap is worked for the same number of rows as there are heel flap stitches (20 rows and 20 stitches). The first decrease of the heel turn begins 2 stitches past the center of the heel stitches (25% + 2; 12 stitches). One stitch is picked up for every other row along the edge of the heel flap for the gussets (25%; 10 stitches picked up from 20 rows). One stitch is decreased at each gusset every other round until the original number of stitches is reached (100%; 40 stitches). The foot is worked for the desired length, then stitches are decreased at each end of the instep and sole stitches every other round until half the number of stitches remain (50%; 20 stitches). Then the decreases are worked every round until 8 to 16 stitches remain (about 20%). Accomplished sock knitters don't even use patterns—they determine how many stitches are needed for the foot and calculate all the other numbers based on that.

For your first pair of socks, let's follow the conventional top-down construction technique. For this example, we'll use a set of four double-pointed needles. We'll start by casting on stitches for the cuff, work the cuff and leg in rounds to the heel, work the heel flap in rows, shape the heel with short-rows, pick up stitches for the gussets, then decrease the gussets while working in rounds to the toe. We'll shape the toe along the side in a typical wedge style, and finally, finish off the tip with a few Kitchener stitches. The sock in the photograph is a woman's medium (8" [20.5 cm] foot circumference) worked with worsted-weight yarn on size 7 (4.5 mm) needles.

Before you can begin, you need to know your gauge. Just like you've been instructed that if you want a sweater to fit, you need to be sure that your gauge matches the one that's called for in the pattern if you want your socks to fit.

This sock was knitted with worsted-weight yarn at a gauge of 5 stitches to the inch on size 7 needles.

Measuring Gauge

To measure gauge for a sock, cast on 20 to 30 stitches using the recommended needle size. Work in stockinette stitch (or another pattern stitch, if you plan to use one) in the round until the piece measures about 4" (10 cm) from the cast-on edge. Remove the swatch from the needles or loosely bind off the stitches. Lay the swatch on a flat surface. Place a ruler over the swatch and count the number of stitches across and the number of rows down (including fractions of stitches and rows) in the space of 2" (5 cm). Repeat this measurement two or three times on different areas of the swatch to confirm your initial results. If you have more stitches and rows than called for in the instructions, your stitches are too small and you should try again with larger needles; if you have fewer stitches or rows, your stitches are too large and you should try again with smaller needles. Repeat the process until you get the gauge you want.

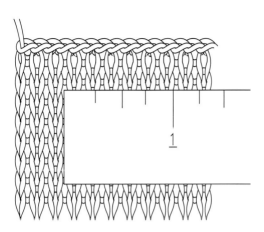

Use a ruler to measure the gauge. This illustration shows a gauge of 6 stitches to the inch. For the most accurate results, measure the gauge over 2" and divide by two to get the number of stitches per inch.

Ways to Knit Socks in Rounds

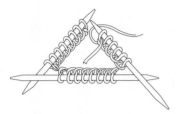

Distribute the stitches between three needles and knit with the fourth.

Four Double-Pointed Needles

Most Americans learn to use four double-pointed needles—the stitches are distributed between three needles and the fourth is used for knitting. For a sock, the stitches are evenly distributed between the three needles while working the leg, but they are rearranged at the heel so that the heel stitches are worked on one needle while the instep stitches are split equally between the other two. After the heel is completed, the stitches are rearranged so that half of the heel stitches are on the first needle, all of the instep stitches are on the second needle, and the remaining half of the heel stitches are on the third needle. The round begins at the back of the leg.

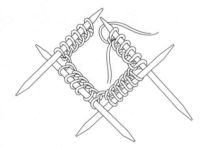

Distribute the stitches between four needles and knit with the fifth.

Five Double-Pointed Needles

Europeans typically learn to knit circularly with five double-pointed needles—the stitches are distributed between four needles and the fifth is used for knitting. For a sock, the stitches are arranged so that the back-of-the-leg, heel, and sole stitches are equally divided between two needles, and the front-of-the-leg and instep stitches are equally divided between the other two. The round begins at the back of the leg.

Place all the stitches on a single short circular needle.

One Very Short Circular Needle

Some needle companies offer 12" (30.5 cm) circular needles that can accommodate the relatively small number of stitches involved in socks. The rigid needle sections at the tips of these needles are quite short and take some getting used to. The advantage of this method is that all the stitches are on a single needle and all you have to do is knit around and around without changing needles, but you'll want to use markers to make sure that the heel and toe stitches are perfectly aligned. The round begins at the side of the leg.

Two Circular Needles

Recently, there has been interest in working socks on two circular needles. The back-of-the-leg, heel, and sole stitches are on one needle and the front-of-the leg and instep stitches are on the other. The round begins at the side of the leg. If you choose this method, you'll want to be careful to keep the stitches and the two needles separate—use each needle only for the stitches that are on that needle. Enthusiasts of this method like the fact that no needle is ever completely empty so it's impossible to lose one; the needle not in use hangs out of the way in back of the work.

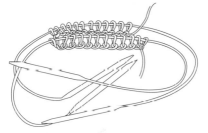

Working with two circular needles.

One Long Circular Needle

Sarah Hauschka recently simplified the method of working socks circularly on a single 40" (100 cm) long circular needle and calls her explanation of the method The Magic Loop. To use this method, cast on the stitches as usual, then slide them to the center of the cable, fold the cable and the stitches exactly at the midpoint, pull a loop of cable out between the two sets of stitches, then slide the stitches to the two needle points. Half of the stitches will be on one needle tip and the other half of the stitches will be on the other tip. Hold the needle tips parallel so that the working yarn comes out of the right-hand edge of the back needle tip. *Pull the back needle tip out to expose about 6" (15 cm) of cable, and use that needle to knit the stitches off of the front needle tip. At the end of those stitches, pull the cable so that the two sets of stitches are at the ends of their respective needle tips again, turn the work around, and repeat from *. In this method there is only one needle to keep track of.

When working socks, the back-of-the-leg, heel, and sole stitches are in one group and the front-of-the-leg and instep stitches are in the other group. The round begins between the two needles (at the side of the leg). If you're doing some type of color work, consider adjusting the needles so that the round begins at the back of the leg. This will position the "jog" or break in the pattern between rounds along the back of the leg and bottom of the foot where it is less obvious.

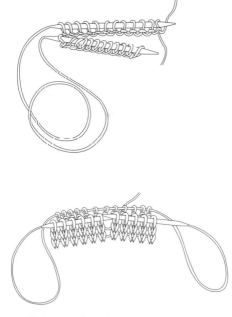

Distribute the stitches between the two tips of the long circular needle, then pull the back needle tip and use it to knit the stitches on the front needle tip.

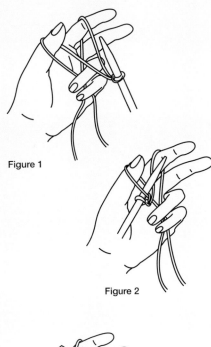

Figure 1

Figure 2

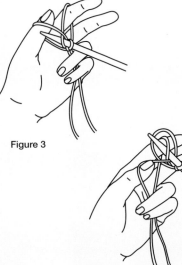

Figure 3

Figure 4

Flexible Cast-Ons

Long-Tail (Continental) Cast-On

The long-tail cast-on forms a sturdy, elastic foundation row. It is worked with two ends of yarn—one that comes from the working ball of yarn and the other that comes from the tail end of that same yarn. Before you can start casting on, though, you need to determine the length of yarn to leave for the tail. To get a good estimate of the length needed for casting on 10 stitches, measure the length of yarn needed to wrap around the needle 10 times. Multiply this length by the number of times that 10 goes into the number of stitches you'll cast on. For example, if it takes 5" (12.5 cm) of yarn to wrap the needle 10 times and you want to cast on 60 stitches, multiply 5" by 6—leave a tail 30" long.

Step 1: Leaving a tail the necessary length, make a slipknot and place it on a needle held in your right hand. The slipknot counts as the first stitch.

Step 2: Place the thumb and index finger of your left hand between the yarn ends so that the strand attached to the ball is around your index finger and the tail end is around your thumb. Secure the yarn ends with your other fingers and hold your palm upwards, making a V of yarn (Figure 1).

Step 3: Bring the needle up through the loop on your thumb (Figure 2).

Step 4: Use the needle to catch the first strand around your index finger, then bring the needle back down through the loop on your thumb (Figure 3).

Step 5: Drop the loop off your thumb and, placing your thumb back in the V configuration, tighten the resulting stitch on needle (Figure 4).

Repeat Steps 3–5 for the desired number of stitches, taking care to leave a bit of horizontal space between stitches to ensure flexibility along the cast-on edge.

Old Norwegian Cast-On

The Old Norwegian cast-on forms a sturdy, very elastic foundation row. It is worked with two ends of yarn—one that comes from the working ball of yarn and the other that comes from the tail end of that same yarn. Before you can start casting on, though, you need to determine the length of yarn to leave for the tail. To get a good estimate of the length needed for casting on 10 stitches, measure the length of yarn needed to wrap around the needle 10 times. Multiply this length by the number of times that 10 goes into the number of stitches you'll cast on. For example, if it takes 5" (12.5 cm) of yarn to wrap the needle 10 times and you want to cast on 60 stitches, multiply 5" by 6—leave a tail 30" long.

Step 1: Leaving a tail the necessary length, make a slipknot and place it on a needle held in your right hand. The slipknot counts as the first stitch.

Step 2: Place the thumb and index finger of your left hand between the yarn ends so that the strand connected to the ball is around your index finger and the tail end is around your thumb. Secure the yarn ends with your other fingers and hold your palm upwards, making a V of yarn (Figure 1).

Step 3: Bring the needle in front of your thumb, under both yarns around the thumb, down into the center of the thumb loop, back forward, and over the top of the yarn around your index finger (Figure 2).

Step 4: Use the needle to catch this yarn, then bring the needle back down through the thumb loop (Figure 3), turning your thumb slightly to make room for the needle to pass through.

Step 5: Drop the loop off your thumb (Figure 4) and place your thumb back in the V configuration while tightening up the resulting stitch on the needle (Figure 5).

Repeat Steps 3–5 for the desired number of stitches.

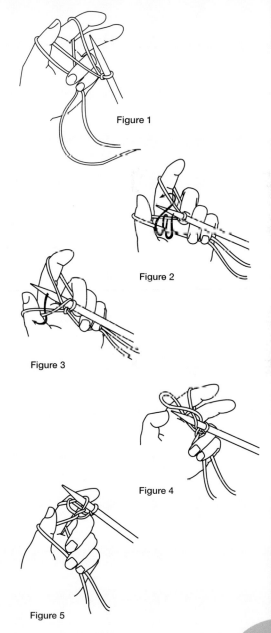

Figure 1

Figure 2

Figure 3

Figure 4

Figure 5

Casting On

For our example here, we'll make a woman's medium sock with worsted-weight yarn at a gauge of 5 stitches to the inch on size 7 (4.5 mm) needles.

To begin, you'll need to get the appropriate number of stitches onto your needles—40 in our case. Regardless of your needle choice, the first step—casting on—is the same. There are a number of cast-on methods, but for socks, you'll want to choose one that is both sturdy and flexible. My two favorite methods are the long-tail (also called the Continental) and the old Norwegian cast-ons (see pages 20 and 21). Both methods involve the interlacing of two yarn ends, which adds stability and strength. Both methods have sufficient give to allow the sock to stretch over your heel.

Step 1: Using the method of your choice, cast on the recommended number of stitches onto a single needle.

Step 2: Distribute the stitches as evenly as possible among three double-pointed needles.

TIP: Ensure a Flexible Cast-On

It's not uncommon for knitters to cast on stitches too tightly in an attempt to create a smooth, firm edge. This can result in socks that bind (and tend to fall down) on the leg or socks that are difficult to pull on around the heel. Although you don't want to err at the opposite extreme, a sock can handle a fairly loose cast-on. Remember that the edge will stretch around your leg so what might look like loose stitches will actually ensure a more comfortable fit.

The long-tail method (see page 20) forms a sturdy edge that works well for socks, provided it is worked loosely enough. Some books suggest working this cast-on over two needles to make a looser edge, but in fact, doing so only makes the first row of stitches larger than the others; it does nothing to add elasticity. To get an edge that has some elasticity, be sure to allow a little space (about ⅛" to ¼" [3 to 6 mm]) between each stitch that is cast on.

My favorite cast-on for socks is the Old Norwegian method (see page 21). Although this method of casting on feels a bit like finger gymnastics while you work it, it produces an edge that is both firm and elastic. I've never had a problem with this method producing a too-tight edge.

Join for Working in the Round

To begin working in rounds, you'll need to join the first cast-on stitch with the last cast-on stitch to form a ring. There are different ways to do this, many of which Nancy Bush describes in *Folk Knitting in Estonia* (Interweave Press, 1999), and three of which are described below.

Ways to Join for Working in Rounds

Simple Join

Just like the name implies, this method is simple. Just start knitting beginning with the first cast-on stitch. There will be a small gap at the join, but this can be effectively tidied up when the cast-on tail is woven in later.

Crossover Join

Step 1: Slip the first cast-on stitch (it will be on the left needle tip) onto the right needle (Figure 1).

Step 2: With the left needle, pick up the last cast-on stitch (now the second stitch on the right needle), bring it up over the top of the previously moved stitch (Figure 2), and place it on the left needle tip (Figure 3).

The first and last stitches have exchanged places and the last stitch cast on surrounds the first.

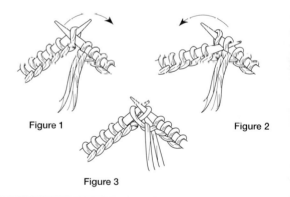

Figure 1

Figure 2

Figure 3

Two-End Join

Work the first two or three stitches of the round with both ends of yarn (the one attached to the ball and the tail end) that were used for the cast-on. After you have worked several stitches, drop the tail end and continue on with the yarn attached to the ball. On the next round, remember that the joining stitches were worked with a double strand of yarn and be sure to work the two strands together as though they were a single stitch.

Most patterns will instruct you to place a marker on the needle when you join for working rounds. This is so you can keep track of where one round ends and the next one begins, and it is especially helpful if you're working a color or texture pattern. To prevent the marker from falling off the needle if you're using double-pointed or two circular needles, slip the marker on the needle between the second-to-last and last stitches of the round.

If you're diligent about keeping the stitches on the needles as described on pages 18–19, you can forego the marker and use the cast-on tail hanging from the first round of knitting to keep track of the beginning and end of rounds.

When you join the cast-on stitches for working in rounds, you must be careful not to let the stitches twist or spiral around the needles. Take a minute to ensure that the stitches are all aligned the same way on the needles with the straight edge of the cast-on at the bottom of every needle. If the straight edge wraps around one of the needles, the stitches are said to be twisted and you'll end up knitting a helix. If this happens, the only solution is to rip out all of the stitches and begin again.

Cuff

To prevent the edge from curling, the first inch (or more) of a sock is worked in a non-curling stitch pattern, most commonly a rib. Not only do ribs lie flat, they also have a tendency to draw in (allowing for stretch), which helps to give a sock a snug fit. The draw-in results from the juxtaposition of knit and purl stitches. The more boundaries there are between knit and purl stitches, the greater the draw-in. Single rib, which alternates 1 stitch each of knit and purl, has the greatest amount of draw-in; double rib (alternating 2 stitches each of knit and purl) has less; and triple rib (alternating three stitches each of knit and purl) has even less. My favorite rib for socks alternates 3 knit stitches with 1 purl stitch. The knit stitches dominate, giving this rib the best of both worlds—it lays flat but looks more like plain stockinette stitch.

In our example, we'll work the cuff in double rib for 2" (5 cm).

Single rib   Double rib   Knit 3, purl 1 rib

Leg

Continue working even in stockinette stitch (knit every stitch of every round) until the leg measures the desired length from the cast-on row to the beginning of the heel.

TIP: Prevent a Ladder of Loose Stitches at Needle Boundaries

Many knitters are plagued by columns of loose stitches between the last stitch on one needle and the first stitch on the next. This typically happens when the first or last stitch on each needle is worked a little looser than the rest. To avoid this problem, maintain consistent tension at needle changes. If this doesn't take care of the problem, shift the boundary between needles every round or two so that the needle boundaries do not fall between the same pair of stitches for more than a couple of rounds. Another solution is to eliminate the boundaries between needles — work the socks on a very short circular needle so that all the stitches are on the same needle. Most knitters find that working with two circular needles or one very long circular needle also eliminates the problem (see pages 18–19).

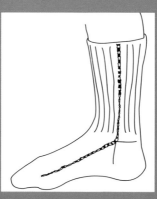

Heel Flap

The heel flap is the extra bit of knitting that extends along the back of the heel from the ankle bone to the base of the foot. For our sock, the heel flap is worked back and forth in rows on half of the total number of stitches. Rearrange the stitches, if necessary, so that all of the heel stitches are on one needle (the other half of the stitches will be worked later for the instep). Work the heel stitches back and forth in rows as follows.

Row 1: (RS) *Sl 1 purlwise with yarn in back (wyb), k1; rep from *.

Row 2: (WS) Sl 1 purlwise with yarn in front (wyf), purl to end.

Repeat Rows 1 and 2 for the specified number of rows, ending with a wrong-side row so that the next row will be a right-side row. For our example, we'll work the heel flap for a total of 20 rows—there will be 10 elongated stitches in the main fabric of the flap and 10 chain selvedge stitches.

Heel Flap Stitches

Standard Slip 1, Knit 1

The standard slip 1, knit 1 (sl 1, k1) stitch was used for the heel flaps in this book, but you can substitute other stitches. Below are a couple of examples.

Reversed Slip 1, Knit 1

This is similar to the standard pattern, but the yarn is held on the right side of the knitting when the stitches are slipped.

Row 1: (WS) Sl 1 purlwise with yarn in back, purl to end.

Row 2: (RS) *Sl 1 purlwise with yarn in front, k1; rep from *.

Repeat Rows 1 and 2 for pattern.

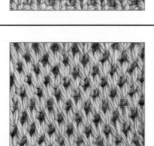

Alternating Slip 1, Knit 1

The stitches that are slipped alternate from row to row, brick fashion. This is commonly called "eye of partridge."

Rows 1 and 3. (WS) Sl 1 purlwise with yarn in front, purl to end.

Row 2: (RS) *Sl 1 purlwise with yarn in back, k1; rep from *.

Row 4: Sl 1 purlwise with yarn in back, k2, *sl 1 purlwise with yarn in back, k1; rep from * to last st, k1.

Repeat Rows 1–4 for pattern.

TIP: Matching Leg and Foot Lengths

Do you ever wonder how knitters make two socks exactly the same size? The secret is in counting rows. This is the best way to be assured that the second sock will be a perfect mate to the first. I use the markers that look like tiny safety pins to mark every 10 or 20 rounds as I work the leg and foot. Then it's a simple matter to count markers to make the second sock match the first.

Heel Turn

You're now ready to work the magical part of a sock—the heel turn. The instructions are basically the same, no matter what size sock you're knitting. The heel is shaped with short-rows, which are nothing more than partial ("short") rows worked on just the center stitches. This causes the center area to have more rows of knitting, making it longer than the edges, which causes that magical cup shape. Work the short-rows as follows.

Row 1: (RS) Knit to 2 stitches beyond the center of the heel stitches (in our example, we have 20 heel stitches, so we'll knit across 12 of them), ssk (see Glossary, page 133), k1 (Figure 1).

Row 2: (WS) Sl 1 purlwise wyf, p5, p2tog, p1 (Figure 2).

Row 3: (RS) Sl 1 purlwise with yarn in back (wyb), knit to 1 stitch before the gap formed on the previous row (in our example, we'll knit 6 stitches), ssk (1 stitch from each side of the gap), k1 (Figure 3).

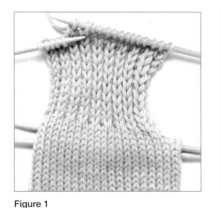

Figure 1

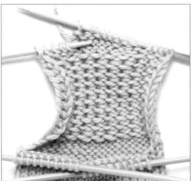

Figure 2

Figure 3

Row 4: (WS) Sl 1 purlwise wyf, purl to 1 stitch before the gap formed on the previous row (in our example, we'll purl 7 stitches), p2tog (1 stitch from each side of the gap), p1 (Figure 4).

Rows 5–8: Repeat Rows 3 and 4 two more times—12 heel stitches will remain on the needle (Figure 5).

If you have more heel stitches to begin with, you'll repeat Short-Rows 3 and 4 until no gaps remain and you've reached to the selvedge edges of the stitches. If you began the heel flap with a number of stitches divisible by 4 (i.e., 16, 20, 24), there will be a single knit stitch after the gap at the end of the last right-side row or a single purl stitch after the gap at the end of the last wrong-side row. That's okay—just work the last two stitches together as usual, without working the k1 or p1 after the decrease, then turn the work and knit a RS row.

Figure 4

Figure 5

Ways to Pick Up and Knit Along Gussets

There are different ways to pick up stitches along the edges of the heel flap to form the gussets. Typically, picking up both loops or picking up through the back loops forms a firmer edge.

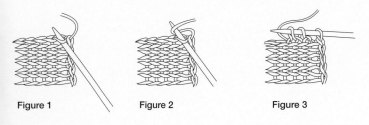

Figure 1   Figure 2   Figure 3

Pick Up a Single Loop

For very little bulk along the pick-up edge, pick up gusset stitches through the front half of the edge stitches. Insert the knitting needle under the front half of the selvedge stitch (Figure 1), wrap the yarn around the needle as if to knit (Figure 2), and bring the wrap through to create a new stitch on the needle. Repeat this for every chain edge stitch (Figure 3).

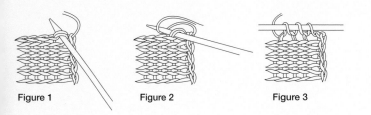

Figure 1   Figure 2   Figure 3

Pick Up Both Loops

For a sturdier join along the pick-up edge, pick up the gusset stitches through both halves of the edge stitch (Figure 1), wrap the yarn around the needle as if to knit (Figure 2), and bring the wrap through to create a new stitch on the needle. Repeat this for every chain edge stitch (Figure 3).

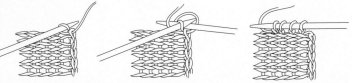

Figure 1   Figure 2   Figure 3

Pick Up Through the Back Loops

For a very snug join, pick up the gusset stitches by working into the back loop of either the first half or both halves of each edge stitch. This is easiest if you work it with two knitting needles. Use the needle in your left hand to lift the back half of the selvedge stitch, then insert the right needle into the back half of the lifted stitch (Figure 1), wrap the yarn around the right needle as if to knit (Figure 2), and bring the wrap through to create a new stitch on the needle. Repeat this for every chain selvedge stitch (Figure 3). For an even tighter join, work through both halves of the selvedge stitches.

Gussets

The next step is to connect the heel with the instep so that you can work the foot in rounds to the tip of the toe. To form the gussets, you'll create new stitches along the sides of the heel flap that will connect the newly turned heel stitches with the waiting instep stitches. This is called "pick up and knit."

Pick Up and Knit Gusset Stitches

Working from right to left, insert a needle tip under the edge stitch, wrap the yarn around the needle, then pull the needle (and wrapped loop) through to the right side (see box on page 30). Because you slipped the first stitch of every row while working the heel flap, the edge stitches are large and easy to recognize.

TIP: Prevent Holes at Gussets

Small holes often form where the instep meets the gussets. As the heel flap is knitted and the gusset stitches are picked up, the stitches at the edges of the instep are subjected to a lot of stress, causing them to become enlarged at the expense of their neighbors. These enlarged stitches are most pronounced if the instep stitches are held on a knitting needle while the heel is worked. To help reduce the problem, use a length of waste yarn (which is flexible) instead of a needle (which is not) to hold the instep stitches while you work the heel. It also helps if you pick up an extra stitch right at the boundary between the instep and heel flap, then work that stitch together with the instep stitch

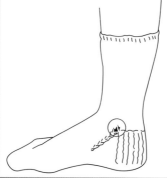

on the next round. Or do what I do—thread a bit of yarn on a tapestry needle and use it to tighten up the hole on the wrong side after the sock is finished (see page 46).

Figure 1

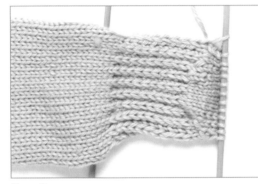
Figure 2

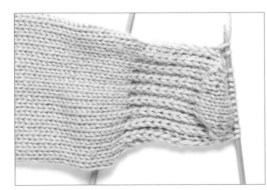
Figure 3

Step 1: With the right side facing and working with the needle holding the heel stitches (Needle 1), pick up and knit the closest chain stitch along the selvedge edge of the heel flap (Figures 1 and 2).

Then pick up 1 stitch in each of the following chain stitches to the end of the heel flap (Figures 3 and 4). In our case, all 10 gusset stitches have been picked up with Needle 1.

Figure 4

Step 2: With a new needle (Needle 2), knit across all of the instep stitches (Figure 5; 20 stitches in our case).

Step 3: With another new needle (Needle 3), pick up and knit 1 stitch in each chain stitch along the other selvedge edge of the heel flap. In our case, this will be 10 stitches (Figure 6). With the same needle, knit the first 6 heel stitches from Needle 1 again (Figure 7).

There will be 52 stitches total—16 stitches on Needle 1 (6 heel stitches plus 10 picked-up gusset stitches), 20 instep stitches on Needle 2, and 16 stitches on Needle 3 (10 picked-up gusset stitches plus 6 heel stitches). We are now ready to work in rounds; the round now begins at the center of the heel stitches.

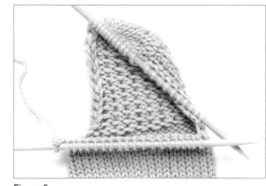

Figure 5

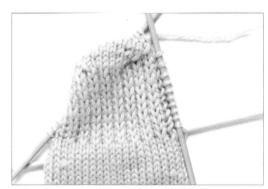

Figure 6

Figure 7

Decrease Gusset Stitches

It's now time to shape the gussets. We will decrease 1 gusset stitch on each side of the instep stitches every other row until we're back to our original number of stitches—40.

Round 1: On Needle 1, knit to the last 3 stitches (Figure 1), knit the next 2 stitches together (k2tog; Figure 2), then knit the last stitch on Needle 1 (Figure 3).

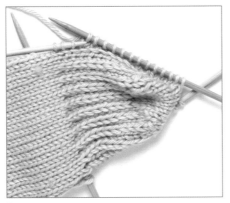

Figure 1

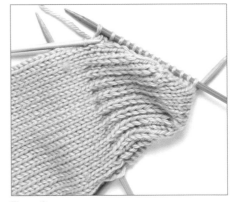

Figure 2

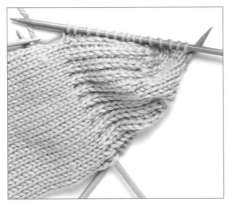

Figure 3

Figure 4

Knit across all the instep stitches on Needle 2 (Figure 4).

On Needle 3, knit 1 stitch (Figure 5), slip the next 2 stitches individually knitwise, then knit them together through their back loops (ssk; see Glossary, page 133; Figure 6), then knit to the end of Needle 3 (Figure 7). This brings us to the end of the round. We've decreased 1 stitch each on Needle 1 and Needle 3, so 15 stitches remain on each heel needle; 50 stitches total.

Round 2: Knit all stitches on all needles.

Repeat Rounds 1 and 2 until 10 stitches remain each on Needle 1 and Needle 3. Because you didn't decrease any instep stitches, there are still 20 stitches on Needle 2; 40 stitches total.

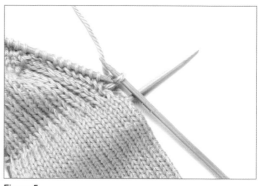

Figure 5

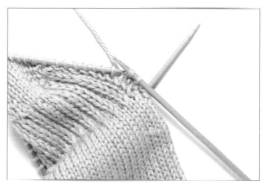

Figure 6

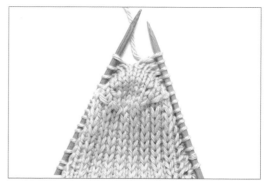

Figure 7

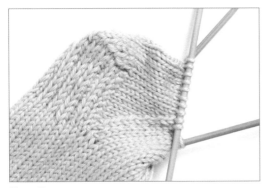

Figure 8

The gusset decreases will form pronounced diagonal stitch lines between the beginning of the heel flap and the foot. When all gusset stitches have been decreased, there will be the same number of stitches as were cast on to begin the leg (Figure 8).

TIP: Proper-Fitting Sock Legs

A proper-fitting sock leg stands up without binding. Most knitters reason that if their socks fall down, they must be too big. Interestingly, the opposite is often the case. If the circumference is too small, the leg will shift and settle around the narrower part of the ankle. An easy fix for this is one I learned from expert knitter Priscilla Gibson-Roberts that I use regularly. Simply knit the upper part of the leg on needles one size larger than those used to get gauge. For most people, the slight increase in gauge will accommodate the increased leg circumference at the calf.

Another reason that sock legs fall down is that they have no elasticity. This is fine if you want slouch socks, but otherwise, choose a yarn that contains a percentage of elastic or work the entire leg in a ribbed pattern. Remember that the more shifts between knit and purl stitches in the rib, the snugger the fit (for example, a knit 1, purl 1 rib has more elasticity than a knit 2, purl 2 rib).

Sock sizes are typically based on the circumference of the widest part of your foot, with the assumption that the cir-

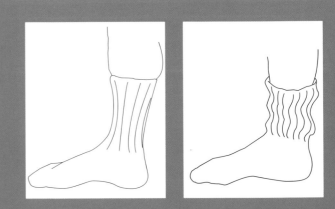

cumference of your leg at the top of the sock will be about the same. If your leg is larger around than your foot, you may want to base your sock size on your leg circumference instead. Choose the size that most closely matches your leg circumference (where the top of the sock will fit). To get the foot to fit, work the foot for fewer rows so that the extra width will stretch into extra length when the sock is worn. Alternatively, work more rows of gusset decreases to reduce the number of stitches to match your foot circumference.

Getting Started Knitting Socks

Foot

Now it's just a matter of knitting around and around until the foot is the desired length to the beginning of the toe shaping. In our case, we'll knit until the piece measures 7½" (19 cm) from the back of the heel, ending the round at the center of the bottom of the foot.

TIP: Preventing Holes in the Heel and Toe

Both the heel and toe of a sock are subjected to a lot of friction as they rub against the inside of a shoe. The first step in prevention is to make sure that the socks are long enough that the stitches aren't stretched too tightly over the toes and heels. The second step is to use a yarn that contains some nylon, which is much more resistant to abrasion than pure wool. If your yarn doesn't contain nylon, add a strand of reinforcing yarn (available at yarn shops) while you work the heel and toe, or when the sock is finished, weave the reinforcing yarn in and out of the purl bumps on the inside of heel or toe as shown at right. If you take none of these precautions, you can always use the duplicate stitch (see Glossary, page 133) to darn the holes if and when they appear.

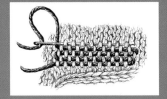

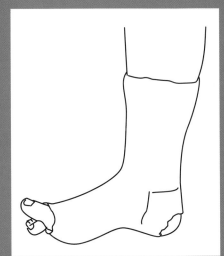

TIP: Socks that Don't Fit

If your socks turn out too small or too big, you either miscalculated your gauge or misjudged the sock size. Be sure to knit your gauge swatch in the round in the stitch pattern you plan to use and be sure to measure the fullest part of your foot when determining size. For the most flexible fit, work the leg and instep in a ribbed pattern that can stretch to accommodate small size variations. If these precautions fail and your socks are too small, you might be able to salvage them by ripping out the toes and knitting the feet a little longer. Because stitches stretch both widthwise and lengthwise, you can gain some extra width by adding extra length. Try on the socks before you start the toe decreases to make sure that you've added enough length to compensate for the narrow width. If your socks are too big, try the opposite—compensate for the extra width by working a shorter foot. If you used wool yarn (but not the superwash kind), try shrinking the socks by running them through the washing machine and dryer or by vigorously felting them by hand with hot soapy water. Be careful, though; once yarn begins to felt there's no going back so be sure to check the progress often. If all this fails, give the socks to a friend who has the right size feet. Your generosity will feel good on both of you.

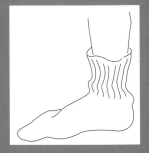

Toe

There are many ways to shape the toe of a sock. The toe we'll work here is called a wedge toe. That's because it forms a wedge shape, with the decreases all worked along the sides of the foot. Check out the books listed in the Bibliography on page 135 for other methods.

Round 1: On Needle 1, knit to the last 3 stitches (Figure 1), knit 2 stitches together (Figure 2), then knit the last stitch of the needle (Figure 3)—there are now 9 stitches on Needle 1.

On Needle 2, knit the first stitch (Figure 4), ssk (Figure 5), knit to the last 3 stitches (Figure 6), k2tog (Figure 7), knit the last stitch of the needle (Figure 8)—there are now 18 stitches on Needle 2.

On Needle 3, knit the first stitch (Figure 9), ssk (Figure 10), knit to the end of the needle (Figure 11).

Round 2: Knit all the stitches on all of the needles

Figure 1

Figure 2

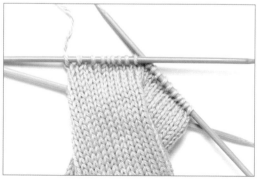

Figure 3

Repeat Rounds 1 and 2 until half of the original number of stitches remain. In our case that will be 20 stitches—5 stitches each on Needle 1 and Needle 3; 10 stitches on Needle 2. Then repeat Row 1 only (decrease every round) until 8 stitches remain. There will be 2 stitches each on Needle 1 and Needle 3 and 4 stitches on Needle 2.

You're nearly done! All that's left is to close off the tip of the toe. My favorite technique is to use the Kitchener stitch to graft the remaining live stitches together. The Kitchener stitch is worked with the yarn threaded

Figure 4

Figure 5

Figure 6

Figure 7

on a tapestry needle to connect the live stitches together, following a path that mimics a row of knitting. This technique has developed a bad reputation for being difficult and confusing. But don't let the naysayers sway you—it's really quite logical. If you just don't feel up to the Kitchener stitch, you can turn the socks inside out and use the three-needle method to bind off the two sets of stitches together, or simply gather the remaining stitches with a length of yarn as described in the box on page 45.

Figure 8

Figure 9

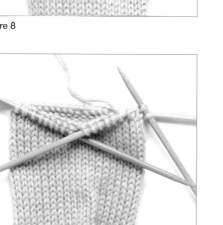

Figure 10

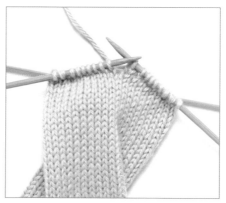

Figure 11

Kitchener Stitch

To begin, the stitches must be arranged so that there are the same number of stitches on each of the two needles and so that the boundaries between the needles are aligned with the sides of the foot. Hold the needles parallel to each other with the right sides of the knitting facing up.

Allowing about ½" (1.3 cm) per stitch to be grafted, thread yarn on a tapestry needle. Work from right to left as follows.

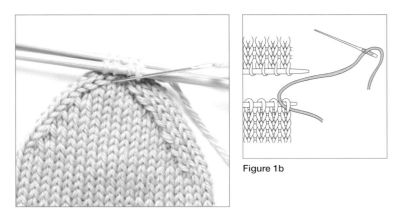

Figure 1b

Step 1. Bring the tapestry needle through the first stitch on the front needle from right to left (as if to purl; Figure 1a) and leave the stitch on the needle (Figure 1b).

Figure 1a

Figure 2b

Step 2. Bring the tapestry needle through the first stitch on the back needle from left to right (as if to knit; Figure 2a) and leave that stitch on the needle (Figure 2b).

Figure 2a

Step 3. Bring the tapestry needle through the first front stitch as if to knit (Figure 3a) and slip this stitch off the needle, then bring the tapestry needle through the next front stitch as if to purl and leave this stitch on the needle (Figure 3b).

Figure 3a

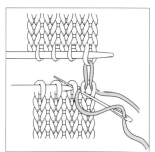

Figure 3b

Step 4. Bring the tapestry needle through the first back stitch as if to purl (Figure 4a) and slip this stitch off the needle, then bring the tapestry needle through the next back stitch as if to knit and leave this stitch on the needle (Figure 4b).

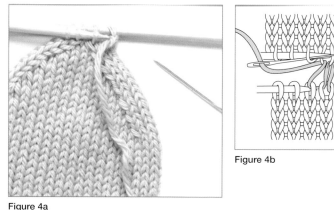

Figure 4a

Figure 4b

Repeat Steps 3 and 4 until no stitches remain on the needles, adjusting the tension to match the rest of the knitting as you go.

To remember all of the steps of this technique, I simply bring the tapestry needle through the first stitch on the front needle purlwise, then through the first stitch on the back needle knitwise, then I mentally chant the following as I work to the end of the stitches.

Front Needle: Insert knitwise in the first stitch and slip it off the needle; insert purlwise in the next stitch and leave it in place.

Back Needle: Insert purlwise in the first stitch and slip it off the needle; insert knitwise in the next stitch and leave it in place.

When you finish, insert the needle into the inside of the sock and weave in the tail on the wrong side (Figures 5 and 6).

Figure 5

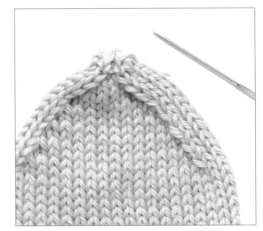

Figure 6

Other Ways to Finish Toes

Three-Needle Bind-Off

Place the stitches to be joined onto two separate needles. Hold the needles so that the right sides of knitting face together. Insert a third needle into the first stitch on each of the other two needles (Figure 1) and knit them together as one stitch (Figure 2), *knit the next stitch on each needle together in the same way, then pass the first stitch over the second and off the needle (Figure 3). Repeat from * until 1 stitch remains on the third needle. Cut yarn and pull the tail through the last stitch.

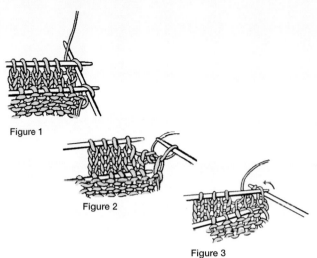

Figure 1

Figure 2

Figure 3

Gathered Tip

Cut the yarn leaving a 10" (25.5 cm) tail, thread the tail on a tapestry needle, run the needle through all of the remaining stitches (Figure 1), pull the yarn tight to close the hole (Figure 2), and fasten if off on the wrong side of the sock

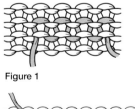

Figure 1

Figure 2

Finishing

Although no one would blame you if you want to put your socks on and dance out the door, they're not really finished until you've taken care of the pesky loose ends, closed up any holes along the heel and gussets, and blocked them.

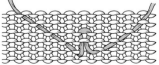

Figure 1

Weave in Loose Ends

The loose ends are the tails of yarn left hanging at the beginning of the cuff, tip of the toe, and possibly elsewhere along the leg, heel, and foot when you had to join a new ball of yarn. Thread the end on a tapestry needle and work it into the wrong side of the sock. You can trace the path of a row of stitches (Figure 1) or work on the diagonal, catching the back side of the stitches (Figure 2).

Figure 2

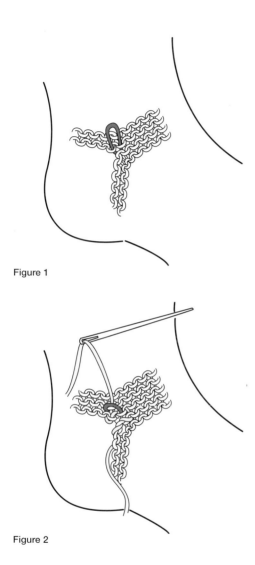

Figure 1

Figure 2

Close Holes at the Gussets

I'd lie if I said that my socks never had holes or gaps at the beginning of the gusset. Over time I've learned ways to minimize these (see box on page 38), but when they do show up, I simply turn the sock inside out and use a piece of yarn to tidy up the offending area. I pull on the enlarged stitch (or stitches) to bring the extra yarn to the inside of the sock (Figure 1), then use a separate length of yarn threaded on a tapestry needle to secure it in place (Figure 2), striving not to distort the stitches on the right side of the sock.

Blocking

Blocking is the final step. Adding moisture to the knitting will even out the lines of stitches and the fibers in the yarn.

Damp Method: My favorite method is to lay the socks on a towel on a flat surface, spray them with water, pat them into shape, and leave them to air-dry.

Sock Blocker Method: Sock blockers are flat forms (usually made of wood) cut to the shape of a foot. Place the finished socks on the blockers, spray them with water, and hang them or lay them flat to air-dry.

Washing Machine Method: If you used yarn that is specified as machine washable (check the ball band carefully), you can simply throw the socks in the washing machine along with a load of clothes of similar color and wash them on the normal cycle. Some yarns are machine dryable, but I usually just take the socks out of the washer and lay them flat to air-dry.

3

Basic
Sock Instructions

The basic instructions are for
working socks at five different
gauges—4, 5, 6, 7, and 8
stitches to the inch.

The instructions that follow are for knitting socks with five different weights of yarn, from fingering to chunky—each in five different sizes. No matter which yarn you want to use or which foot you want to fit, you'll have the right instructions. All you have to do is choose a yarn and work a gauge swatch for that yarn (see page 17), then choose a size and follow the instructions for your gauge in that size.

These instructions are for socks worked from the cuff down to the toe, with a ribbed leg and a stockinette stitch foot. The projects that follow in Chapters 4–6 are all based on these instructions. As you'll find in Chapters 5 and 6, it's a small matter to add color or texture patterns, change the length of the leg, or the shape of the cuff.

Choosing a Size

The best way to determine what size to make your sock is to measure your foot. Wrap a tape measure around the widest part of your foot, pulling the tape snug, but not tight (Figure 1). This is your foot circumference, which is the most important measurement in a sock. The lengths of the leg and foot are proportional to the foot circumference and are based on this measurement. But if

The basic instructions are for working socks at five sizes ranging from child's medium to adult large.

you want to control the exact dimensions of your socks, you can take these measurements, too. To measure your foot length, lay a ruler on the floor and lightly step on it, placing your heel at the "0" and measuring the length to your longest toe (Figure 2). To measure your leg length, stand next to a wall and hold a ruler against the wall with the "0" on the floor and measure how high up your leg you want the sock to extend (Figure 3).

If you're knitting socks for a gift and can't take these measurements, that's okay. The instructions in this book are based on five standard foot circumferences that range from child to adult sizes. You can also use shoe size as a guide for sock size. For reasons I'll never understand, sock sizes do not match shoe sizes. But because socks stretch, there is a lot of leeway in sizing. See the table on page 51 for conversions between U.S. shoe sizes, total foot length, and the sock sizes provided in this book. If you know the size shoes you (or your friends) wear, you can make socks that will fit.

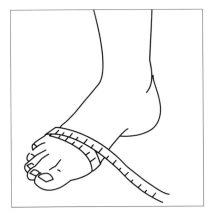

Figure 1

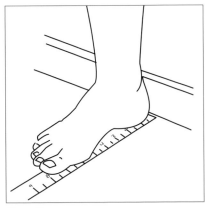

Figure 2

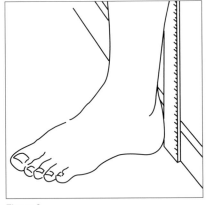

Figure 3

For the most part, a sock should be snug. It should hug your foot but not feel binding. Your toes should be free to move but not swimming in excess fabric. The foot should be tight enough that it doesn't shift or twist as you walk and the leg should be snug without binding. I like to plan for my socks to be about ½" (1.3 cm) shorter than my total foot length. That way, the stitches stretch slightly to give me a snug fit.

You can custom fit a sock by adding or subtracting length. For example, if you wear U.S. woman's size 8 shoes, you may want to make your socks a little shorter than the 10¼" (26 cm) specified in the instructions. Conversely, if you wear size 10 shoes, you might want to knit your socks a tad longer. If you have wide feet, consider following the instructions for a larger size, but shorten the length. Try the opposite if you have narrow feet.

The basic patterns that follow are for working with four double-pointed needles; see pages 18–19 for other options.

What Size Sock Should You Knit?

U.S. Shoe Size	Total Foot Length	Sock Size in This Book
Children's 9–12	7" (18 cm)	child medium
Children's 1–4	8¼" (21 cm)	child large
Women's 5–7/Men's 4–6	9½" (24 cm)	adult small
Women's 8–10/Men's 7–9	10¼" (26 cm)	adult medium
Women's 11–14/Men's 10–13	11" (29 cm)	adult large

8 Stitches Per Inch
#1 Super Fine; fingering weight

Finished Size

About 6½ (7½, 8, 9, 9¾)" (16.5 [19, 20.5, 23, 25] cm) foot circumference and about 7 (8¼, 9½, 10¼, 11)" (18 [21, 24, 26, 28] cm) foot length from back of heel to tip of toe. To fit child medium (child large, adult small, adult medium, adult large); see page 51 for shoe size conversions.

Yarn

Fingering weight (#1 Super Fine; see page 12): About 236 (322, 384, 477, 564) yd (216 [294, 351, 436, 516] m).

Needles

Size US 0–3 (2–3.25 mm), as necessary to obtain 8 stitches/inch in St st.

Leg

CO 52 (60, 64, 72, 76) sts. Join for working in rnds, being careful not to twist sts. Work patt of choice until leg measures 5½ (6½, 7, 8, 8¾)" (14 [16.5, 18, 20.5, 22] cm) from CO, or desired length to top of heel.

Heel

K13 (15, 16, 18, 19), turn work around and with same needle p26 (30, 32, 36, 38)—26 (30, 32, 36, 38) heel sts on one needle. Place rem 26 (30, 32, 36, 38) sts on spare needle(s) or holder to work later for instep.

Heel Flap

Work back and forth on heel sts in rows as foll:

Row 1: (RS) *Sl 1 pwise with yarn in back (wyb), k1; rep from *.

Row 2: Sl 1 pwise with yarn in front (wyf), purl to end.

Rep Rows 1 and 2 until a total of 26 (30, 32, 36, 38) rows have been worked—13 (15, 16, 18, 19) chain selvedge sts.

Turn Heel

Work short-rows as foll:

Row 1: (RS) K15 (17, 18, 20, 21), ssk, k1, turn work.

Row 2: (WS) Sl 1 pwise, p5, p2tog, p1, turn.

Row 3: Sl 1 pwise, knit to 1 st before gap made on previous row, ssk (1 st from each side of gap), k1, turn.

Row 4: Sl 1 pwise, purl to 1 st before gap made on previous row, p2tog (1 st from each side of gap; see Glossary, page 133), p1, turn.

Repeat Rows 3 and 4 until all heel sts have been worked, ending with a WS row and ending the last repeat as ssk on Row 3 and p2tog on Row 4 if there are not enough sts to work the final k1 or p1 after the final dec (i.e., if you began the heel with 32 or 36 sts)—16 (18, 18, 20, 22) sts rem.

Gusset

Note: One extra st is picked up along the selvedge in the corner of each heel flap to avoid leaving a hole at the base of the gusset. Rejoin for working in the rnd as foll:

Rnd 1: With one needle (Needle 1), knit across all heel sts, then pick up and knit 14 (16, 17, 19, 20) sts along selvedge edge of heel flap; with another needle (Needle 2), work across 26 (30, 32, 36, 38) held instep sts; with another needle (Needle 3), pick up and knit 14 (16, 17, 19, 20) sts along other side of heel flap, then knit across the first 8 (9, 9, 10, 11) heel sts from Needle 1 again—70 (80, 84, 94, 100) sts total; 22 (25, 26, 29, 31) sts each on Needle 1 and Needle 3; 26 (30, 32, 36, 38) instep sts on Needle 2. Rnd now begins at center back heel.

Rnd 2: On Needle 1, knit to last 3 sts, k2tog, k1; on Needle 2, knit across all instep sts; on Needle 3, k1, ssk, knit to end—2 gusset sts dec'd.

Rnd 3: Knit.

Rep Rnds 2 and 3 until 52 (60, 64, 72, 76) sts rem—13 (15, 16, 18, 19) sts each on Needle 1 and Needle 3; 26 (30, 32, 36, 38) instep sts on Needle 2.

Foot

Work even until piece measures 5½ (6½, 7½, 8, 8¾)" (14 [16.5, 19, 20.5, 22] cm) from back of heel, or about 1½ (1¾, 2, 2¼, 2¼)" (3.8 [4.5, 5, 5.5, 5.5] cm) less than desired total foot length.

Toe

Rnd 1: On Needle 1, knit to last 3 sts, k2tog, k1; on Needle 2, k1, ssk, work to last 3 sts, k2tog, k1; on Needle 3, k1, ssk, knit to end—4 sts dec'd.

Rnd 2: Knit.

Rep Rnds 1 and 2 until 24 (28, 32, 36, 40) sts rem. Rep Rnd 1 *only* until 8 (12, 12, 16, 16) sts rem. Knit sts from Needle 1 onto Needle 3—4 (6, 6, 8, 8) sts each on 2 needles.

Finishing

Cut yarn, leaving an 18" (45.5 cm) tail. Using the Kitchener st (see pages 42–44), graft sts tog. Weave in loose ends. Block.

7 Stitches Per Inch
#1 Super Fine or #2 Fine; fingering or sportweight

Finished Size

About 6½ (7½, 8, 9, 9¾)" (16.5 [19, 20.5, 23, 25] cm) foot circumference and about 7 (8¼, 9½, 10¼, 11)" (18 [21, 24, 26, 28] cm) foot length from back of heel to tip of toe. To fit child medium (child large, adult small, adult medium, adult large); see page 51 for shoe size conversions.

Yarn

Fingering weight or sportweight (#1 Super Fine or #2 Fine; see page 12): About 215 (293, 349, 434, 513) yd (197 [268, 319, 397, 469] m).

Needles

Size US 0–3 (2–3.25 mm), as necessary to obtain 7 stitches/inch in St st.

Leg

CO 44 (52, 56, 64, 68) sts. Join for working in rnds, being careful not to twist sts. Work patt of choice until leg measures 5½ (6½, 7, 8, 8¾)" (14 [16.5, 18, 20.5, 22] cm) from CO, or desired length to top of heel.

Heel

K11 (13, 14, 16, 17), turn work around and with same needle, p22 (26, 28, 32, 34)—22 (26, 28, 32, 34) heel sts on one needle. Place rem 22 (26, 28, 32, 34) sts on spare needle(s) or holder to work later for instep.

Heel Flap

Work back and forth on heel sts in rows as foll:

Row 1: (RS) *Sl 1 pwise with yarn in back (wyb), k1; rep from *.

Row 2: Sl 1 pwise with yarn in front (wyf), purl to end.

Rep Rows 1 and 2 until a total of 22 (26, 28, 32, 34) rows have been worked—11 (13, 14, 16, 17) chain selvedge sts.

Turn Heel

Work short-rows as foll:

Row 1: (RS) K13 (15, 16, 18, 19), ssk, k1, turn work.

Row 2: (WS) Sl 1 pwise, p5, p2tog, p1, turn.

Row 3: Sl 1 pwise, knit to 1 st before gap made on previous row, ssk (1 st from each side of gap; see Glossary, page 133), k1, turn.

Row 4: Sl 1 pwise, purl to 1 st before gap made on previous row, p2tog (1 st from each side of gap), p1, turn.

Repeat Rows 3 and 4 until all heel sts have been worked, ending with a WS row and ending the last repeat as ssk on Row 3 and p2tog on Row 4 if there are not enough sts to work the final k1 or p1 after the final dec (i.e., if you began the heel with 28 or 32 sts)—14 (16, 16, 18, 20) sts rem.

Gusset

Note: One extra st is picked up along the selvedge in the corner of each heel flap to avoid leaving a hole at the base of the gusset. Rejoin for working in the rnd as foll:

Rnd 1: With one needle (Needle 1), knit across all heel sts, then pick up and knit 12 (14, 15, 17, 18) sts along selvedge edge of heel flap; with another dpn (Needle 2), work across 22 (26, 28, 32, 34) held instep sts; with another dpn (Needle 3), pick up and knit 12 (14, 15, 17, 18) sts along other side of heel flap, then knit across the first 7 (8, 8, 9, 10) heel sts from Needle 1 again—60 (70, 74, 84, 90) sts total; 19 (22, 23, 26, 28) sts each on Needle 1 and Needle 3; 22 (26, 28, 32, 34) instep sts on Needle 2. Rnd now begins at center back heel.

Rnd 2: On Needle 1, knit to last 3 sts, k2tog, k1; on Needle 2, knit across all instep sts; on Needle 3, k1, ssk, knit to end—2 gusset sts dec'd.

Rnd 3: Knit.

Rep Rnds 2 and 3 until 44 (52, 56, 64, 68) sts rem—11 (13, 14, 16, 17) sts each on Needle 1 and Needle 3; 22 (26, 28, 32, 34) instep sts on Needle 2.

Foot

Work even until piece measures 5½ (6½, 7½, 8, 8¾)" (14 [16.5, 19, 20.5, 22] cm) from back of heel, or about 1½ (1¾, 2, 2¼, 2¼)" (3.8 [4.5, 5, 5.5, 5.5] cm) less than desired total foot length.

Toe

Rnd 1: On Needle 1, knit to last 3 sts, k2tog, k1; on Needle 2, k1, ssk, work to last 3 sts, k2tog, k1; on Needle 3, k1, ssk, knit to end—4 sts dec'd.

Rnd 2: Knit.

Rep Rnds 1 and 2 until 20 (24, 28, 32, 36) sts rem. Rep Rnd 1 *only* until 8 (8, 8, 12, 12) sts rem. Knit sts from Needle 1 onto Needle 3—4 (4, 4, 6, 6) sts each on 2 needles.

Finishing

Cut yarn, leaving an 18" (45.5 cm) tail. Using the Kitchener st (see pages 42–44), graft sts tog. Weave in loose ends. Block.

6 Stitches Per Inch
#2 Fine or #3 Light; sportweight or DK weight

Finished Size

About 6½ (7½, 8, 9, 9¾)" (16.5 [19, 20.5, 23, 25] cm) foot circumference and about 7 (8¼, 9½, 10¼, 11)" (18 [21, 24, 26, 28] cm) foot length from back of heel to tip of toe. To fit child medium (child large, adult small, adult medium, adult large); see page 51 for shoe size conversions.

Yarn

Sportweight or DK weight (#2 Fine or #3 Light; see page 12): About 195 (266, 317, 394, 466) yd (179 [243, 290, 361, 426] m).

Needles

Size US 2–4 (2.75–3.5 mm), as necessary to obtain 6 stitches/inch in St st.

Leg

CO 40 (44, 48, 52, 56) sts. Join for working in rnds, being careful not to twist sts. Work patt of choice until leg measures 5½ (6½, 7, 8, 8¾)" (14 [16.5, 18, 20.5, 22] cm) from CO, or desired length to top of heel.

Heel

K10 (11, 12, 13, 14), turn work around and with same needle, p20 (22, 24, 26, 28)—20 (22, 24, 26, 28) heel sts on one needle. Place rem 20 (22, 24, 26, 28) sts on spare needle(s) or holder to work later for instep.

Heel Flap

Work back and forth on heel sts in rows as foll:

Row 1: (RS) *Sl 1 pwise with yarn in back (wyb), k1; rep from *.

Row 2: Sl 1 pwise with yarn in front (wyf), purl to end.

Rep Rows 1 and 2 until a total of 20 (22, 24, 26, 28) rows have been worked—10 (11, 12, 13, 14) chain selvedge sts.

Turn Heel

Work short-rows as foll:

Row 1: (RS) K12 (13, 14, 15, 16), ssk, k1, turn work.

Row 2: (WS) Sl 1 pwise, p5, p2tog, p1, turn.

Row 3: Sl 1 pwise, knit to 1 st before gap made on previous row, ssk (1 st from each side of gap; see Glossary, page 133), k1, turn.

Row 4: Sl 1 pwise, purl to 1 st before gap made on previous row, p2tog (1 st from each side of gap), p1, turn.

Repeat Rows 3 and 4 until all heel sts have been worked, ending with a WS row and ending the last repeat as ssk on Row 3 and p2tog on Row 4 if there are not enough sts to work the final k1 or p1 after the final dec (i.e., if you began the heel with 20, 24, or 28 sts)—12 (14, 14, 16, 16) sts rem.

Gusset

Note: One extra st is picked up along the selvedge in the corner of each heel flap to avoid leaving a hole at the base of the gusset. Rejoin for working in the rnd as foll:

Rnd 1: With one needle (Needle 1), knit across all heel sts, then pick up and knit 11 (12, 13, 14, 15) sts along selvedge edge of heel flap; with another dpn (Needle 2), work across 20 (22, 24, 26, 28) held instep sts; with another dpn (Needle 3), pick up and knit 11 (12, 13, 14, 15) sts along other side of heel flap, then knit across the first 6 (7, 7, 8, 8) heel sts from Needle 1 again—54 (60, 64, 70, 74) sts total; 17 (19, 20, 22, 23) sts each on Needle 1 and Needle 3; 20 (22, 24, 26, 28) instep sts on Needle 2.

Rnd now begins at center back heel.

Rnd 2: On Needle 1, knit to last 3 sts, k2tog, k1; on Needle 2, knit across all instep sts; on Needle 3, k1, ssk, knit to end—2 gusset sts dec'd.

Rnd 3: Knit.

Rep Rnds 2 and 3 until 40 (44, 48, 52, 56) sts rem—10 (11, 12, 13, 14) sts each on Needle 1 and Needle 3; 20 (22, 24, 26, 28) instep sts on Needle 2.

Foot

Work even until piece measures 5½ (6½, 7½, 8, 8¾)" (14 [16.5, 19, 20.5, 22] cm) from back of heel, or about 1½ (1¾, 2, 2¼, 2¼)" (3.8 [4.5, 5, 5.5, 5.5] cm) less than desired total foot length.

Toe

Rnd 1: On Needle 1, knit to last 3 sts, k2tog, k1; on Needle 2, k1, ssk, work to last 3 sts, k2tog, k1; on Needle 3, k1, ssk, knit to end—4 sts dec'd.

Rnd 2: Knit.

Rep Rnds 1 and 2 until 20 (20, 24, 28, 28) sts rem. Rep Rnd 1 *only* until 8 sts rem for all sizes. Knit sts from Needle 1 onto Needle 3—4 sts each on 2 needles.

Finishing

Cut yarn, leaving an 18" (45.5 cm) tail. Using the Kitchener st (see pages 42–45), graft sts tog. Weave in loose ends. Block.

5 Stitches Per Inch

#4 Medium; worsted weight

Finished Size

About 6½ (7½, 8, 9, 9¾)" (16.5 [19, 20.5, 23, 25] cm) foot circumference and about 7 (8¼, 9½, 10¼, 11)" (18 [21, 24, 26, 28] cm) foot length from back of heel to tip of toe. To fit child medium (child large, adult small, adult medium, adult large); see page 51 for shoe size conversions.

Yarn

Worsted weight (#4 Medium; see page 12): About 138 (188, 224, 279, 329) yd (126 [172, 205, 255, 301] m).

Needles

Size US 4–8 (3.5–5 mm), as necessary to obtain 5 stitches/inch in St st.

Leg

CO 32 (36, 40, 44, 48) sts. Join for working in rnds, being careful not to twist sts. Work patt of choice until leg measures 5½ (6½, 7, 8, 8¾)" (14 [16.5, 18, 20.5, 22] cm) from CO, or desired length to top of heel.

Heel

K8 (9, 10, 11, 12), turn work around and with same needle, p16 (18, 20, 22, 24)—16 (18, 20, 22, 24) heel sts on one needle. Place rem 16 (18, 20, 22, 24) sts on spare needle(s) or holder to work later for instep.

Heel Flap

Work back and forth on heel sts in rows as foll:

Row 1: (RS) *Sl 1 pwise with yarn in back (wyb), k1; rep from *.

Row 2: Sl 1 pwise with yarn in front (wyf), purl to end.

Rep Rows 1 and 2 until a total of 16 (18, 20, 22, 24) rows have been worked—8 (9, 10, 11, 12) chain selvedge sts.

Turn Heel

Work short-rows as foll:

Row 1: (RS) K10 (11, 12, 13, 14), ssk, k1, turn work.

Row 2: (WS) Sl 1 pwise, p5, p2tog, p1, turn.

Row 3: Sl 1 pwise, knit to 1 st before gap made on previous row, ssk (1 st from each side of gap; see Glossary, page 133), k1, turn.

Row 4: Sl 1 pwise, purl to 1 st before gap made on previous row, p2tog (1 st from each side of gap), p1, turn.

Repeat Rows 3 and 4 until all heel sts have been worked, ending with a WS row and ending the last repeat as ssk on Row 3 and p2tog on Row 4 if there are not enough sts to work the final k1 or p1 after the final dec (i.e., if you began the heel with 16, 20, or 24 sts)—10 (12, 12, 14, 14) sts rem.

Gusset

Note. One extra st is picked up along the selvedge in the corner of each heel flap to avoid leaving a hole at the base of the gusset. Rejoin for working in the rnd as foll:

Rnd 1: With one needle (Needle 1), knit across all heel sts, then pick up and knit 9 (10, 11, 12, 13) sts along selvedge edge of heel flap; with another dpn (Needle 2), work across 16 (18, 20, 22, 24) held instep sts; with another dpn (Needle 3), pick up and knit 9 (10, 11, 12, 13) sts along other side of heel flap, then knit across the first 5 (6, 6, 7, 7) heel sts from Needle 1 again—44 (50, 54, 60, 64) sts total; 14 (16, 17, 19, 20) sts each on Needle 1 and Needle 3; 16 (18, 20, 22, 24) instep sts on Needle 2. Rnd now begins at center back heel.

Rnd 2: On Needle 1, knit to last 3 sts, k2tog, k1; on Needle 2, knit across all instep sts; on Needle 3, k1, ssk, knit to end—2 gusset sts dec'd.

Rnd 3: Knit.

Rep Rnds 2 and 3 until 32 (36, 40, 44, 48) sts rem—8 (9, 10, 11, 12) sts each on Needle 1 and Needle 3; 16 (18, 20, 22, 24) instep sts on Needle 2.

Foot

Work even until piece measures 5½ (6½, 7½, 8, 8¾)" (14 [16.5, 19, 20.5, 22] cm) from back of heel, or about 1½ (1¾, 2, 2¼, 2¼)" (3.8 [4.5, 5, 5.5, 5.5] cm) less than desired total foot length.

Toe

Rnd 1: On Needle 1, knit to last 3 sts, k2tog, k1; on Needle 2, k1, ssk, work to last 3 sts, k2tog, k1; on Needle 3, k1, ssk, knit to end—4 sts dec'd.

Rnd 2: Knit.

Rep Rnds 1 and 2 until 16 (16, 20, 20, 24) sts rem. Rep Rnd 1 *only* until 8 sts rem for all sizes. Knit sts from Needle 1 onto Needle 3—4 sts each on 2 needles.

Finishing

Cut yarn, leaving an 18" (45.5 cm) tail. Using the Kitchener st (see pages 42–45), graft sts tog. Weave in loose ends. Block.

4 Stitches Per Inch
#5 Bulky; chunky weight

Finished Size
About 6½ (7½, 8, 9, 9¾)" (16.5 [19, 20.5, 23, 25] cm) foot circumference and about 7 (8¼, 9½, 10¼, 11)" (18 [21, 24, 26, 28] cm) foot length from back of heel to tip of toe. To fit child medium (child large, adult small, adult medium, adult large); see page 51 for shoe size conversions.

Yarn
Chunky weight (#5 Bulky; see page 12): About 125 (170, 202, 252, 296) yd (115 [156, 185, 231, 271] m).

Needles
Size US 8–11 (5–8 mm), as necessary to obtain 4 stitches/inch in St st.

Leg
CO 24 (28, 32, 36, 40) sts. Join for working in rnds, being careful not to twist sts. Work patt of choice until leg measures 5½ (6½, 7, 8, 8¾)" (14 [16.5, 18, 20.5, 22] cm) from CO, or desired length to top of heel.

Heel
K6 (7, 8, 9, 10), turn work around and with same needle, p12 (14, 16, 18, 20)—12 (14, 16, 18, 20) heel sts on one needle. Place rem 12 (14, 16, 18, 20) sts on spare needle(s) or holder to work later for instep.

Heel Flap
Work back and forth on heel sts in rows as foll:

Row 1: (RS) *Sl 1 pwise with yarn in back (wyb), k1; rep from *.

Row 2: Sl 1 pwise with yarn in front (wyf), purl to end.

Rep Rows 1 and 2 until a total of 12 (14, 16, 18, 20) rows have been worked—6 (7, 8, 9, 10) chain selvedge sts.

Turn Heel

Work short-rows as foll:

Row 1: (RS) K8 (9, 10, 11, 12), ssk, k1, turn work.

Row 2: (WS) Sl 1 pwise, p5, p2tog, p1, turn.

Row 3: Sl 1 pwise, knit to 1 st before gap made on previous row, ssk (1 st from each side of gap; see Glossary, page 133), k1, turn.

Row 4. Sl 1 pwise, purl to 1 st before gap made on previous row, p2tog (1 st from each side of gap), p1, turn.

Repeat Rows 3 and 4 until all heel sts have been worked, ending with a WS row and ending the last repeat as ssk on Row 3 and p2tog on Row 4 if there are not enough sts to work the final k1 or p1 after the final dec (i.e., if you began the heel with 12, 16, or 20 sts)—8 (10, 10, 12, 14) sts rem.

Gusset

Note. One extra st is picked up along the selvedge in the corner of each heel flap to avoid leaving a hole at the base of the gusset. Rejoin for working in the rnd as foll:

Rnd 1: With one needle (Needle 1), knit across all heel sts and pick up and knit 7 (8, 9, 10, 11) sts along selvedge edge of heel flap; with another needle (Needle 2), work across 12 (14, 16, 18, 20) held instep sts; with another needle (Needle 3), pick up and knit 7 (8, 9, 10, 11) sts along other side of heel flap, then knit across the first 4 (5, 5, 6, 6) heel sts from Needle 1 again—34 (40, 44, 50, 54) sts total; 11 (13, 14, 16, 17) sts each on Needle 1 and Needle 3; 12 (14, 16, 18, 20) instep sts on Needle 2. Rnd now begins at center back heel.

Rnd 2: On Needle 1, knit to last 3 sts, k2tog, k1; on Needle 2, knit across all instep sts; on Needle 3, k1, ssk, knit to end—2 gusset sts dec'd.

Rnd 3: Knit.

Rep Rnds 2 and 3 until 24 (28, 32, 36, 40) sts rem—6 (7, 8, 9, 10) sts each on Needle 1 and Needle 3; 12 (14, 16, 18, 20) instep sts on Needle 2.

Foot

Work even until piece measures 5½ (6½, 7½, 8, 8¾)" (14 [16.5, 19, 20.5, 22] cm) from back of heel, or about 1½ (1¾, 2, 2¼, 2¼)" (3.8 [4.5, 5, 5.5, 5.5] cm) less than desired total foot length.

Toe

Rnd 1: On Needle 1, knit to last 3 sts, k2tog, k1; on Needle 2, k1, ssk, work to last 3 sts, k2tog, k1; on Needle 3, k1, ssk, knit to end—4 sts dec'd.

Rnd 2: Knit.

Rep Rnds 1 and 2 until 12 (16, 16, 20, 20) sts rem. Rep Rnd 1 *only* until 8 sts rem for all sizes. Knit sts from Needle 1 onto Needle 3—4 sts each on 2 needles.

Finishing

Cut yarn, leaving an 18" (45.5 cm) tail. Using the Kitchener st (see pages 42–45), graft sts tog. Weave in loose ends. Block.

4

Color and Texture the Easy Way

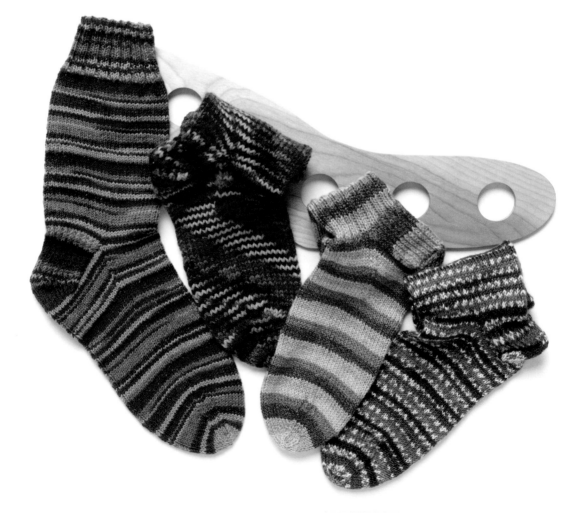

As satisfying as it can be to knit a plain-colored sock, the fun really begins when you add color and texture. But that doesn't have to add difficulty. There are dozens of yarns available that do this for you as you knit a basic pattern.

Yarns come pre-dyed to make all sorts of patterns show up when they're knitted into socks—splotches of color, stripes, zigzags, even Fair Isle look-alikes. Some of these yarns are manufactured specifically for sock knitting; others are intended for more general use.

The way the colors in self-patterning yarn appear when knitted depends on the number of stitches on the needles, your gauge, and the length of the separate colors in the yarn. If the yarn is dyed with long lengths of color, you're likely to get stripes. If the yarn is dyed with shorter lengths of colors, you're likely to get splotches or zigzags. If the yarn is dyed with a combination of long and short lengths of color, you can get patterns that look like Fair Isle. Imagine, all those color changes without having to join new balls of yarn.

The best way to know how one of these yarns will knit up is to knit a swatch. But be aware that what you see in a swatch of 20 stitches will not necessarily look the same as a sock knitted on 40 stitches. To know exactly how the yarn is going to look in your sock, you'll need to knit a swatch with the same number of stitches you plan to use in your sock (and, of course, you'll need to knit that swatch in the round, too). In other words, you won't really know until you knit your socks. But this isn't a bad thing. I love watching the pattern emerge on my needles, never knowing for certain what the next round will look like. As long as I like the colors in the ball of yarn, I know I'm going to like the socks that come out of it.

Even if you prefer solid-colored socks, you can add texture simply by choosing a textured yarn. Choose a soft fuzzy yarn for warm slipper socks. Keep in mind that fuzzy yarns make it harder to see individual stitches so knitting socks with these yarns can be more of a challenge, but they feel oh, so good.

Wide Stripes Socks

This cotton/wool yarn is comfortable for year-round wear. The yarn is dyed to produce wide, even stripes. The entire leg is ribbed and the foot is worked in stockinette stitch. Look closely at the stripe pattern on the two socks and you'll notice that the color sequence is tan/gold/red/blue in one sock and blue/red/gold/tan in the other. I started each sock using yarn pulled for the center of a new ball of yarn to produce matching socks (or so I thought), but the color sequence was reversed for the second ball—the two skeins must have been wound in opposite directions at the factory! This is the kind of serendipity that makes working with self-patterning yarns so much fun (and so hard to duplicate).

Finished Size

About 6½ (7½, 8, 9, 9¾)" (16.5 [19, 20.5, 23, 25] cm) foot circumference and about 7 (8¼, 9½, 10¼, 11)" (18 [21, 24, 26, 28] cm) foot length from back of heel to tip of toe. To fit child medium (child large, adult small, adult medium, adult large); see page 51 for shoe size conversions. Sock shown here measures 8" (20.5 cm) foot circumference.

Yarn

Fingering weight (#1 Super Fine; see page 12). *Shown here:* Lana Grossa Meilenweit Cotton Fun & Stripes (45% cotton, 42% wool, 13% polyamide; 208 yd [190 m]/50 g): gold/orange/brown/blue stripes, 2 (2, 2, 3, 3) balls. (This particular color has been discontinued.)

Needles

Size 3 (3.25 mm): set of 4 double-pointed (dpn). Adjust needle size if necessary to obtain the correct gauge.

Notions

Marker (m); tapestry needle.

Gauge

14 stitches and 18 rounds = 2" (5 cm) in stockinette stitch worked in the round.

Leg

CO 44 (52, 56, 64, 68) sts. Place marker and join for working in rnds, being careful not to twist sts. Work even k2, p2 rib until leg measures 5½ (6½, 7, 8, 8¾)" (14 [16.5, 18, 20.5, 22] cm) from CO, or desired length to top of heel.

Heel, Foot, Toe, and Finishing

Complete according to Basic Sock Pattern for 7 stitches/inch (see page 54).

Narrow Stripes Socks

This is another example of self-striping yarn. The lengths of the color bands in this particular yarn vary so that the stripes are of different widths and appear random in sequence. However, the color pattern repeats about every 3" (7.5 cm) to bring an overall sense of order to the pattern. These socks have a single (knit 1, purl 1) rib at the cuff; the rest of the leg and foot are worked in stockinette stitch.

Finished Size

About 6½ (7½, 8, 9, 9¾)" (16.5 [19, 20.5, 23, 25] cm) foot circumference and about 7 (8¼, 9½, 10¼, 11)" (18 [21, 24, 26, 28] cm) foot length from back of heel to tip of toe. To fit child medium (child large, adult small, adult medium, adult large); see page 51 for shoe size conversions. Socks shown measure 9" (23 cm) foot circumference.

Yarn

Fingering weight (#1 Super Fine; see page 12).
Shown here: Regia Stretch Crazy Color (70% wool, 23% nylon, 7% polyester; 219 yd [200 m]/50 g): #113 navy/burgundy mix, 2 (2, 2, 2, 3) balls.

Needles

Size 3 (3.25 mm): set of 4 double-pointed (dpn). Adjust needle size if necessary to obtain the correct gauge.

Notions

Marker (m); tapestry needle.

Gauge

14 stitches and 22 rounds = 2" (5 cm) in stockinette stitch worked in the round.

Leg

CO 44 (52, 56, 64, 68) sts. Place marker and join for working in rnds, being careful not to twist sts. Work k2, p2 rib until piece measures 1½ (1¾, 2, 2, 2¼)" (3.8 [4.5, 5, 5, 5.5] cm) from CO. Cont even in St st until leg measures 5½ (6½, 7, 8, 8¾)" (14 [16.5, 18, 20.5, 22] cm) from CO, or desired length to top of heel.

Heel, Foot, Toe, and Finishing

Complete according to Basic Sock Pattern for 7 stitches/inch (see page 54).

Spiral Stripes Socks

In yarns dyed with color bands that are not long enough to accommodate all of the stitches in a round, the colors shift to produce a spiral effect. The number of stitches on the needles will affect how tightly the spiral twists—the more stitches, the shallower the twist. Notice how the patterns are different on the two socks. I worked each sock with the same number of stitches and pulled the yarn from the center of a new ball for each. This is another example of how hard it is know what the yarn will look like until you knit it up—even with two balls of the same dyelot. These socks have a single (knit 1, purl 1) rib at the cuff; the rest of the leg and foot are worked in stockinette stitch.

Finished Size

About 6½ (7½, 8, 9, 9¾)" (16.5 [19, 20.5, 23, 25] cm) foot circumference and about 7 (8¼, 9½, 10¼, 11)" (18 [21, 24, 26, 28] cm) foot length from back of heel to tip of toe. To fit child medium (child large, adult small, adult medium, adult large); see page 51 for shoe size conversions. Socks shown measure 8" (20.5 cm) foot circumference.

Yarn

Worsted weight (#4 Medium; see page 12).
Shown here: Lion Brand Lion Wool Prints (100% wool; 143 yd [131 m]/2 oz [78 g]): #201 autumn sunset, 2 (2, 2, 3, 3) balls.

Needles

Size 8 (5 mm): set of 4 double-pointed (dpn). Adjust needle size if necessary to obtain the correct gauge.

Notions

Marker (m); tapestry needle.

Gauge

10 stitches and 14 rounds = 2" (5 cm) in stockinette stitch worked in the round.

Leg

CO 32 (36, 40, 44, 48) sts. Place marker and join for working in rnds, being careful not to twist sts. Work k1, p1 rib until piece measures 1½ (1¾, 2, 2, 2¼)" (3.8 [4.5, 5, 5, 5.5] cm) from CO. Cont even in St st until leg measures 5½ (6½, 7, 8, 8¾)" (14 [16.5, 18, 20.5, 22] cm) from CO, or desired length to top of heel.

Heel, Foot, Toe, and Finishing

Complete according to Basic Sock Pattern for 5 stitches/inch (see page 58).

Magic Stripes Socks

This sock looks like it involves a lot of tricky color changes, but that's due to the way the yarn is dyed. Relatively long bands of color alternate with very short spots that knit up to produce alternating stripes and speckles. The short cuff is worked in a double rib (knit 2, purl 2), then the rest of the leg and foot are worked in stockinette stitch.

Finished Size

About 6½ (7½, 8, 9, 9¾)" (16.5 [19, 20.5, 23, 25] cm) foot circumference and about 7 (8¼, 9½, 10¼, 11)" (18 [21, 24, 26, 28] cm) foot length from back of heel to tip of toe. To fit child medium (child large, adult small, adult medium, adult large); see page 51 for shoe size conversions. Socks shown measure 8" (20.5 cm) foot circumference.

Yarn

Fingering weight (#1 Super Fine; see page 12).
Shown here: Lion Brand Magic Stripes (75% superwash wool, 25% nylon; 330 yd [302 m]/100 g): #203 purple, 1 (1, 2, 2, 2) ball(s).

Needles

Upper leg—size 3 (3.25 mm): set of 4 double-pointed (dpn). Lower leg and foot—size 2 (2.75 mm): set of 4 dpn. Adjust needle size if necessary to obtain the correct gauge.

Notions

Marker (m); tapestry needle

Gauge

16 stitches and 20 rounds = 2" (10 cm) in stockinette stitch worked in the round on smaller needles.

Leg

With larger needles, CO 52 (60, 64, 72, 76) sts. Place marker and join for working in rnds, being careful not to twist sts.

Cuff

Work k2, p2 ribbing until piece measures 1½ (1½, 1¾, 1¾, 2)" (3.8 [3.8, 4.5, 4.5, 5] cm) from CO.

Leg

Change to smaller needles and work in St st until piece measures 5½ (6½, 7, 8, 8¾)" (14 [16.5, 18, 20.5, 22] cm) from CO.

Heel, Foot, Toe, and Finishing

Complete according to Basic Sock Pattern for 8 stitches/inch (see page 52).

Bouclé Socks

Acrylic bouclé yarn gives a lush, cozy texture to these thick slipper socks. The entire leg is worked in double (knit 2, purl 2) rib and the foot is worked in stockinette stitch. Yarns this textured tend to obscure the stitches and make it difficult to see stitches and count rows, especially in the heel flap. You may want to use a row counter to help you keep track of the number of rows you've knitted.

Finished Size

About 6½ (7½, 8, 9, 9¾)" (16.5 [19, 20.5, 23, 25] cm) foot circumference and about 7 (8¼, 9½, 10¼, 11)" (18 [21, 24, 26, 28] cm) foot length from back of heel to tip of toe. To fit child medium (child large, adult small, adult medium, adult large); see page 51 for shoe size conversions. Socks shown measure 8" (20.5 cm) foot circumference.

Yarn

Chunky weight (#5 Bulky; see page 12).
Shown here: TLC Amoré Solid (80% acrylic, 20% nylon; 278 yd [254 m]/6 oz [170 g]): #3782 garnet, 1 (1, 1, 1, 2) skein(s).

Needles

Size 7 (4.5 mm): set of 4 double-pointed. Adjust needle size if necessary to obtain the correct gauge.

Notions

Marker; tapestry needle.

Gauge

8 stitches and 12 rounds = 2" (5 cm) in stockinette stitch worked in the round.

Leg

CO 24 (28, 32, 36, 40) sts. Place marker and join for working in rnds, being careful not to twist sts. Work k2, p2 rib until leg measures 5½ (6½, 7, 8, 8¾)" (14 [16.5, 18, 20.5, 22] cm) from CO, or desired length to top of heel.

Heel, Foot, Toe, and Finishing

Complete according to Basic Sock Pattern for 4 stitches/inch (see page 60), working foot and toe in St st.

5

Adding Your Own Color or Texture Pattern

Once you're familiar with the basics of sock knitting, it's a small step to add your own color or texture patterns. From manly ribs to girly lace, you can give your socks just about any personality. Try out one of the stripe, ribbing, cable, or lace patterns shown on the following pages or choose another from any of the reference books of pattern stitches (see Bibliography, page 135).

You can add color or texture patterns on the cuff, leg, or instep. In general, it's not a good idea to add texture patterns to the bottom of the foot where they can cause uncomfortable bumps. I often like to extend the pattern all around the leg and along the top of the instep so that the pattern shows whether my shoes are on or off.

The most important thing to remember is to take your gauge measurement on the stitch pattern you plan to use so that your sock will turn out the size you want. For example, if you plan to add a cable pattern, you'll want to make sure that you account for the draw-in of the cable crosses, which tend to narrow the width. Conversely, lace patterns can stretch widthwise. Rib patterns stretch to fit the curve of your leg and foot and are a good choice if you're uncertain about the exact size to make.

If you want to work a pattern around the sock leg, either at the cuff or all the way down the leg to the heel, make sure that the number of stitches in the pattern repeat fits evenly into the number of stitches you'll be casting on. The instructions for the basic socks are all a multiple of four stitches, so stitch patterns that repeat over two or four stitches will work with all the basic patterns. Depending on the size of the sock and gauge, patterns that repeat over different numbers of stitches may work as well.

If you want to continue a pattern along the instep, plan ahead to make sure that it's centered over the stitches that will form the front of the leg and instep. This is easiest to do if you choose a pattern that fits evenly into the half the number of stitches that you cast on. For example, if you cast on 40 stitches for the leg, the instep will be worked on 20 stitches and you'll want to choose a pattern that fits evenly into those stitches; the remaining 20 stitches will be worked for the bottom of the foot in stockinette stitch. Sometimes, you'll want to add or subtract a pattern stitch or two to balance the pattern over the instep. For example, if you're working a knit 3, purl 1 rib over the 20 stitches of the instep, you can add an extra purl 1 at the beginning of the sequence or remove the last purl 1 so that the two edges of the pattern look the same (either purl 1 at each edge or knit 3 at each edge). To do this, I might work a different number of stitches in the instep pattern than I work in stockinette stitch for the bottom of the foot. That is, I

might work 21 stitches in the instep pattern as a repeating pattern of purl 1, knit 3, and end with purl 1 at the other end. In this case, I'd work 19 stitches in stockinette stitch for the bottom of the foot.

Stripe Patterns

Stripes are a fun way to add color without having to worry about stitch counts and pattern repeats. And, if the stripes are worked in stockinette stitch, you can work them around the entire foot. To change colors, simply leave a 4" (10 cm) tail to weave in later and begin knitting with the new color. You can change colors as often as you like to make wide or narrow stripes that repeat (or don't repeat) in a uniform or random sequence. To get an idea how a color sequence will look in the yarns you've chosen, wrap the yarns around a ruler or knitting needle, allowing each wrap to represent a row of knitting.

Wrap yarn around a ruler (or knitting needle) to experiment with different stripe sequences.

Fibonacci Stripes Socks

One of my favorite stripe sequences is based on the Fibonacci series, where you begin with the numbers 1 and 2, then add the last two numbers of the series together to come up with the next. For example, the first 6 numbers of the series are 1, 2, 3, 5, 8, and 13. For working stripes, knit the specified number of rounds with one color, then the next specified number of rounds with a different color, etc. The three pairs of socks shown here are three variations of the same color theme—I rotated three colors among four units of the series (2, 3, 5, and 8).

These socks follow the basic pattern for 7 stitches/inch (see page 54) and are worked on four double-pointed needles.

Finished Size

About 6½ (7½, 8, 9, 9¾)" (16.5 [19, 20.5, 23,
25] cm) foot circumference and about 7 (8¼, 9½,
10¼, 11)" (18 [21, 24, 26, 28] cm) foot length from
back of heel to tip of toe. To fit child medium (child
large, adult small, adult medium, adult large); see
page 51 for shoe size conversions. Socks shown
all measure 8" (20.5 cm) foot circumference.

Yarn

Sportweight (#2 Fine; see page 12).
Shown here: Louet Gems Sport Weight (100%
wool; 225 yd [206 m]/100 g): 1 skein each of 3
colors for all sizes.
Colorway 1: Tobacco (A), aqua (B), mustard (C).
Colorway 2: Terra cotta (A), burgundy (B), citrus
orange (C).
Colorway 3: Sage (A), French blue (B), grape (C).

Needles

Upper leg—size 4 (3.5 mm): set of 4 double
pointed (dpn). Lower leg and foot—size 3
(3.25 mm): set of 4 dpn. Adjust needle size if
necessary to obtain the correct gauge.

Notions

Marker; tapestry needle.

Gauge

14 stitches and 18 rounds = 2" (5 cm) in stockinette stitch worked in the round on smaller
needles.

Stitch Guide

Color Pattern (multiple of 33 rnds)

*Work 2 rnds A, 3 rnds B, 5 rnds C, 1 rnd A,
2 rnds B, 3 rnds C, 5 rnds A, 1 rnd B, 2 rnds C,
3 rnds A, 5 rnds B, 1 rnd C; rep from * for pattern.

Leg

With A and larger needles, CO 44 (52, 56, 64, 68) sts. Place marker and join for working in rnds, being careful not to twist sts. Working k3, p1 rib, work even in color patt (see Stitch Guide) until leg measures 2¾ (3¼, 3½, 4, 4½)" (7 [8.5, 9, 10, 11.5] cm) from CO. Change to smaller needles and cont in rib and color patt until piece measures about 5½ (6½, 7, 8, 8¾)" (14 [16.5, 18, 20.5, 22] cm) from CO, or desired length to top of heel, and end having just finished working 5 rnds with B.

Heel

With C, K11 (13, 14, 16, 17), turn work around and with same needle, p22 (26, 28, 32, 34)—22 (26, 28, 32, 34) heel sts on one needle. Place rem 22 (26, 28, 32, 34) sts on spare needle(s) or holder to work later for instep. *Note:* Rib patt will not be exactly centered on instep sts for all sizes.

Heel Flap

With C, work back and forth on heel sts in rows as foll:

Row 1: (RS) *Sl 1 pwise with yarn in back (wyb), k1; rep from *.

Row 2: Sl 1 pwise with yarn in front (wyf), purl to end.

Rep Rows 1 and 2 until a total of 22 (26, 28, 32, 34) rows have been worked—11 (13, 14, 16, 17) chain selvedge sts.

Turn Heel

With C, work short-rows as foll:

Row 1: (RS) K13 (15, 16, 18, 19), ssk, k1, turn work.

Row 2: (WS) Sl 1 pwise, p5, p2tog, p1, turn.

Row 3: Sl 1 pwise, knit to 1 st before gap made on previous row, ssk (1 st from each side of gap; see Glossary, page 133), k1, turn.

Row 4: Sl 1 pwise, purl to 1 st before gap made on previous row, p2tog (1 st from each side of gap), p1, turn.

Repeat Rows 3 and 4 until all heel sts have been worked, ending with a WS row and ending the last repeat as ssk on Row 3 and p2tog on Row 4 if there are not enough sts to work the final k1 or p1 after the dec—14 (16, 16, 18, 20) sts rem.

Gusset

Note: One extra st is picked up along the selvedge in the corner of each heel flap to avoid leaving a hole at the base of the gusset. With C, rejoin for working in the rnd as foll:

Rnd 1: With one needle (Needle 1), knit across all heel sts, then pick up and knit 12 (14, 15, 17, 18) sts along selvedge edge of heel flap; with another dpn (Needle 2), work across 22 (26, 28, 32, 34) held instep sts in established rib patt; with another dpn (Needle 3), pick up and knit 12 (14, 15, 17, 18) sts along other side of heel flap, then knit across the first 7 (8, 8, 9, 10) heel sts from Needle 1 again—60 (70, 74, 84, 90) sts total; 19 (22, 23, 26, 28) sts each on Needle 1 and Needle 3; 22 (26, 28, 32, 34) instep sts on Needle 2. Rnd now begins at center back heel.

Resume working color patt from the beg with 2 rnds of A foll by 3 rnds of B. *Note:* Socks shown in Colorway 1 are worked differently and beg with the 11th rnd of color patt, starting with 1 rnd of A foll by 2 rnds of B. Cont as foll:

Rnd 2: On Needle 1, knit to last 3 sts, k2tog, k1; on Needle 2, work in rib patt across all instep sts; on Needle 3, k1, ssk, knit to end—2 gusset sts dec'd.

Rnd 3: Knit.

Rep Rnds 2 and 3 until 44 (52, 56, 64, 68) sts rem—11 (13, 14, 16, 17) sts each on Needle 1 and Needle 3; 22 (26, 28, 32, 34) instep sts on Needle 2.

Foot

Work even in established patt until piece measures 5½ (6½, 7½, 8, 8¾)" (14 [16.5, 19, 20.5, 22] cm) from back of heel, or about 1½ (1¾, 2, 2¼, 2¼)" (3.8 [4.5, 5, 5.5, 5.5] cm) less than desired total foot length, and end having just finished working 5 rnds with A. *Note:* Socks shown in Color away 1 end with 5 rnds of B.

Toe

Change to C for Colorway 1 and B for Colorways 2 and 3, and work all sts in St st as foll:

Rnd 1: On Needle 1, knit to last 3 sts, k2tog, k1; on Needle 2, k1, ssk, knit to last 3 sts, k2tog, k1; on Needle 3, k1, ssk, knit to end—4 sts dec'd.

Rnd 2: Knit.

Rep Rnds 1 and 2 until 20 (24, 28, 32, 36) sts rem. Rep Rnd 1 *only* until 8 (8, 8, 12, 12) sts rem. Knit sts from Needle 1 onto Needle 3—4 (4, 4, 6, 6) sts each on 2 needles.

Finishing

Cut yarn, leaving an 18" (45.5 cm) tail. Using the Kitchener st (see pages 42–45), graft sts tog. Weave in loose ends. Block.

Magic Ball Socks

These socks are knitted from five different colors of yarn that were leftover from various other projects. To make a magic ball of yarn, I broke off random lengths of each color in no particular order and used the wet-splice method (see box on page 83) to join the lengths together. Then I just followed the basic pattern for 8 stitches/inch, modified slightly to center the rib pattern along the top of the instep, and knitted up a pair of socks like no other. Easy!

These socks follow the basic pattern for 8 stitches/inch (see page 52) and are worked on four double-pointed needles.

Finished Size

About 6½ (7½, 8, 9, 9¾)" (16.5 [19, 20.5, 23, 25] cm) foot circumference and about 7 (8¼, 9½, 10¼, 11)" (18 [21, 24, 26, 28] cm) foot length from back of heel to tip of toe. To fit child medium (child large, adult small, adult medium, adult large); see page 51 for shoe size conversions. Socks shown measure 8" (20.5 cm) foot circumference.

Yarn

Fingering weight (#1 Super Fine; see page 12): About 236 (322, 384, 477, 564) yd (216 [294, 351, 437, 516] m) total of various yarns spliced together.

Shown here: Koigu Premium Merino (100% merino; 170 yd [155 m]/50 g): mix of 5 colors.

Needles

Upper leg—size 3 (3.25 mm): set of 4 double-pointed (dpn). Lower leg and foot—size 2 (2.75 mm): set of 4 dpn. Adjust needle size if necessary to obtain the correct gauge.

Notions

Marker (m); tapestry needle.

Gauge

16 stitches and 22 rounds = 2" (5 cm) in stockinette stitch worked in the round on smaller needles.

Leg

With larger needles, CO 52 (60, 64, 72, 76) sts. Place marker and join for working in rnds, being careful not to twist sts. Work even in k3, p1 rib until piece measures 2¾ (3¼, 3½, 4, 4½)" (7 [8.5, 9, 10, 11.5] cm) from CO. Change to smaller needles and cont in established rib until piece measures 5½ (6½, 7, 8, 8¾)" (14 [16.5, 18, 20.5, 22] cm) from CO, or desired length to top of heel.

Heel

K11 (15, 15, 19, 19), turn work around and with same needle, p27 (31, 31, 35, 35) and inc 1 st along the way—28 (32, 32, 36, 36) heel sts on one needle. Place rem 25 (29, 33, 37, 41) sts on spare needle(s) or holder to work later for instep; there should be a p1 at each end of instep needle.

Heel Flap

Work back and forth on heel sts in rows as foll:

Row 1: (RS) *Sl 1 pwise with yarn in back (wyb), k1; rep from *.

Row 2: Sl 1 pwise with yarn in front (wyf), purl to end.

Rep Rows 1 and 2 until a total of 26 (30, 32, 36, 38) rows have been worked—13 (15, 16, 18, 19) chain selvedge sts.

Turn Heel

Work short-rows as foll:

Row 1: (RS) K16 (18, 18, 20, 20), ssk, k1, turn work.

Row 2: (WS) Sl 1 pwise, p5, p2tog, p1, turn.

Row 3: Sl 1 pwise, knit to 1 st before gap made on previous row, ssk (1 st from each side of gap; see Glossary, page 133), k1, turn.

Row 4: Sl 1 pwise, purl to 1 st before gap made on previous row, p2tog (1 st from each side of gap), p1, turn.

Repeat Rows 3 and 4 until all heel sts have been worked, ending with a WS row and ending the last repeat as ssk for Row 3 and p2tog for Row 4 if there are not enough sts to work the final k1 or p1 after the dec—16 (18, 18, 20, 20) sts rem.

Gusset

Note: One extra st is picked up along the selvedge in the corner of each heel flap to avoid leaving a hole at the base of the gusset. Rejoin for working in the rnd as foll:

Rnd 1: With one needle (Needle 1), knit across all heel sts, then pick up and knit 14 (16, 17, 19, 20) sts along selvedge edge of heel flap; with another needle (Needle 2), work across 25 (29, 33, 37, 41) held instep sts in established rib patt; with another needle (Needle 3), pick up and knit 14 (16, 17, 19, 20) sts along other side of heel flap, then knit across the first 8 (9, 9, 10, 10) heel sts from Needle 1 again—69 (79, 85, 95, 101) sts total; 22 (25, 26, 29, 30) sts each on Needle 1 and Needle 3; 25 (29, 33, 37, 41) instep sts on Needle 2. Rnd now begins at center back heel.

Rnd 2: On Needle 1, knit to last 3 sts, k2tog, k1; on Needle 2, work all instep sts in established rib patt, beg and ending with p1; on Needle 3, k1, ssk, knit to end—2 gusset sts dec'd.

Rnd 3: Knit all sts on Needle 1 and Needle 3, work instep sts on Needle 2 in established rib.

Rep Rnds 2 and 3 until 53 (61, 65, 73, 77) sts rem—14 (16, 16, 18, 18) sts each on Needle 1 and Needle 3; 25 (29, 33, 37, 41) instep sts on Needle 2. Work 1 rnd even in patt, then dec 1 st as before on Needle 1 *only*—52 (60, 64, 72, 76) sts.

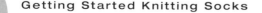

Foot

Work even as established until piece measures 5½ (6½, 7½, 8, 8¾)" (14 [16.5, 19, 20.5, 22] cm) from back of heel, or about 1½ (1¾, 2, 2¼, 2¼)" (3.8 [4.5, 5, 5.5, 5.5] cm) less than desired total foot length.

Toe

Rearrange sts if necessary so there are 13 (15, 16, 18, 19) sts each Needle 1 and Needle 3 and 26 (30, 32, 36, 38) sts on Needle 2. Work all sts in St st as foll:

Rnd 1: On Needle 1, knit to last 3 sts, k2tog, k1, on Needle 2, k1, ssk, work to last 3 sts, k2tog, k1; on Needle 3, k1, ssk, knit to end— 4 sts dec'd.

Rnd 2: Knit.

Rep Rnds 1 and 2 until 24 (28, 32, 36, 40) sts rem. Rep Rnd 1 *only* until 8 (12, 12, 16, 16) sts rem. Knit sts from Needle 1 onto Needle 3—4 (6, 6, 8, 8) sts each on 2 needles.

Finishing

Cut yarn, leaving an 18" (45.5 cm) tail. Using the Kitchener st (see pages 42–45), graft sts tog. Weave in loose ends. Block.

Wet-Splice Yarns

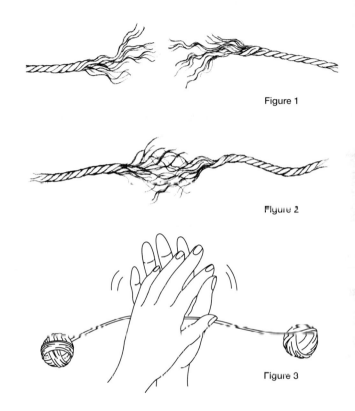

Figure 1

Figure 2

Figure 3

To splice together two balls of yarns, untwist an inch or two from the end of each ball (Figure 1), overlap the raveled ends (Figure 2), moisten them with water (saliva works well and is always available, though not always the most polite). Place the overlapped loose fibers in one palm and use your other palm to vigorously rub the two ends together (Figure 3). The moisture and friction will cause the two yarn ends to felt together. (*Note:* This method only works for yarns that are predominantly wool.)

Rib Patterns

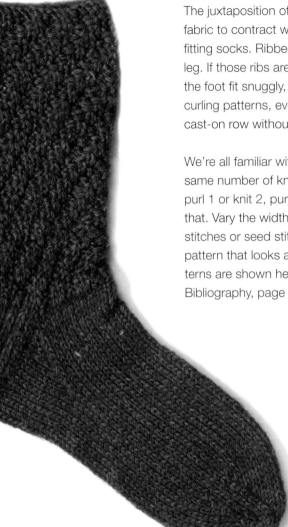

The juxtaposition of columns of knit and purl stitches causes the fabric to contract widthwise, making ribbed patterns ideal for snug-fitting socks. Ribbed patterns help the leg of a sock mold to your leg. If those ribs are continued along the top of the instep, they help the foot fit snuggly, too. Because ribbed patterns are stable, non-curling patterns, even decorative variations can be started at the cast-on row without the need for a cuff pattern.

We're all familiar with the basic ribbed patterns that alternate the same number of knit stitches and purl stitches, for example knit 1, purl 1 or knit 2, purl 2. But there are more interesting patterns than that. Vary the width of the knit or purl columns or add a few garter stitches or seed stitches between the ribs and you can produce a pattern that looks a lot more exciting. Some of my favorite rib patterns are shown here; check out books of stitch patterns (see Bibliography, page 135) for other ideas.

☐	knit
•	purl
℺	k1 through back loop
☐	pattern repeat

4-stitch repeats

Seeded Rib

Garter Rib

1x1 Twisted Rib

Mistake Rib

6-stitch repeats

Twisted Rib Variation

5

3

1

Garter Rib

5

3

1

Moss Rib

5

3

1

See page 84 for symbol key.

Garter Rib Variation

5

3

1

8-stitch repeats

Garter Rib

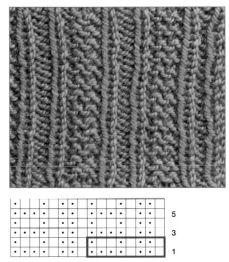

5
3
1

1, 2, 3 Variation

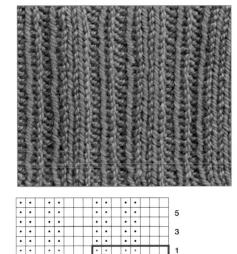

5
3
1

Seed Rib

5
3
1

See page 84 for symbol key.

1, 2 Variation

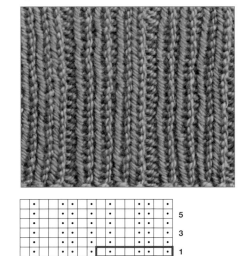

5
3
1

Seeded Rib Socks

The masculine rib pattern on the leg and instep of these socks alternates single knit stitches with 2 purl stitches and 2 seed stitches. The purl stitches tend to recede to make the panels of seed stitch more prominent. This type of rib doesn't draw in as much as traditional knit 1, purl 1 or knit 2, purl 2 ribs, but it has sufficient elasticity for a snug fit. To accommodate full repeats of the 6-stitch pattern, the number of stitches cast-on (and worked for the leg, heel, foot and toes) for some of the sizes deviates from the basic pattern for 6 stitches/inch. This isn't cheating—it's designing!

These socks follow the basic pattern for 6 stitches/inch (see page 56) with modifications and are worked on four double-pointed needles.

Finished Size

About 6½ (7½, 8, 9, 9¾)" (16.5 [19, 20.5, 23, 25] cm) foot circumference and about 7 (8¼, 9½, 10¼, 11)" (18 [21, 24, 26, 28] cm) foot length from back of heel to tip of toe. To fit child medium (child large, adult small, adult medium, adult large); see page 51 for shoe size conversions. Socks shown measure 8" (20.5 cm) foot circumference.

Yarn

Sportweight (#2 Fine; see page 12).
Shown here: Brown Sheep Nature Spun Sport (100% wool; 184 yd [168 m]/50 g): #200 wood moss, 2 (2, 2, 3, 3) skeins.

Needles

Upper leg—size 6 (4 mm): set of 4 double-pointed (dpn). Lower leg and foot—size 5 (3.75 mm): set of 4 dpn. Adjust needle size if necessary to obtain the correct gauge.

Notions

Marker (m); tapestry needle.

Gauge

12 stitches and 16 rounds = 2" (5 cm) in stock-inette stitch worked in the round on smaller needles.

Stitch Guide

Embossed Moss Stitch (multiple of 6 sts)

Rnd 1: *K1, p1, k2, p2; rep from *.
Rnd 2: *K2, p1, k1, p2; rep from *.
Repeat Rounds 1 and 2 for pattern.

Leg

With larger needles, CO 42 (42, 48, 54, 60) sts. Place marker and join for working in rnds, being careful not to twist sts. Work in embossed moss st (see Stitch Guide) until piece measures 2¾ (3¼, 3½, 4, 4½)" (7 [8.5, 9, 10, 11.5] cm) from CO. Change to smaller needles and cont in established rib until piece measures 5½ (6½, 7, 8, 8¾)" (14 [16.5, 18, 20.5, 22] cm) from CO, or desired length to top of heel.

Heel

K10 (11, 11, 10, 11), turn work around and with same needle, sl 1, p21 (17, 23, 27, 29) and dec 2 (inc 2, inc 0, inc 0, inc 0) sts evenly spaced as you go—20 (20, 24, 28, 30) heel sts on one needle. Place rem 20 (24, 24, 26, 30) sts on spare needle(s) or holder to work later for instep; sts at each end of instep needle should be p2 (p1, p1, p2, p1) so the pattern is centered on the instep.

Heel Flap

Work back and forth on heel sts in rows as foll:

Row 1: (RS) *Sl 1 pwise with yarn in back (wyb), k1; rep from *.

Row 2: Sl 1 pwise with yarn in front (wyf), purl to end.

Rep Rows 1 and 2 until a total of 20 (22, 24, 26, 28) rows have been worked—10 (11, 12, 13, 14) chain selvedge sts.

Turn Heel

Work short-rows as foll:

Row 1: (RS) K12 (12, 14, 16, 17), ssk, k1, turn work.

Row 2: (WS) Sl 1 pwise, p5, p2tog, p1, turn.

Row 3: Sl 1 pwise, knit to 1 st before gap made on previous row, ssk (1 st from each side of gap; see Glossary, page 133), k1, turn.

Row 4: Sl 1 pwise, purl to 1 st before gap made on previous row, p2tog (1 st from each side of gap), p1, turn.

Repeat Rows 3 and 4 until all heel sts have been worked, ending with a WS row and ending the last repeat ssk on Row 3 and p2tog on Row 4 if there are not enough sts to work the final k1 or p1 after the dec—12 (12, 14, 16, 18) sts rem.

Gusset

Note: One extra st is picked up along the selvedge in the corner of each heel flap to avoid leaving a hole at the base of the gusset. Rejoin for working in the rnd as foll:

Rnd 1: With one needle (Needle 1), knit across all heel sts, then pick up and knit 11 (12, 13, 14, 15) sts along selvedge edge of heel flap; with another needle (Needle 2), work across 20 (24, 24, 26, 30) held instep sts in established patt; with another needle (Needle 3), pick up and knit 11 (12, 13, 14, 15) sts along other side of heel flap, then knit across the first 6 (6, 7, 8, 9) heel sts from Needle 1 again—54

(60, 64, 70, 78) sts total; 17 (18, 20, 22, 24) sts each on Needle 1 and Needle 3; 20 (24, 24, 26, 30) instep sts on Needle 2. Rnd now begins at center back heel.

Rnd 2: On Needle 1, knit to last 3 sts, k2tog, k1; on Needle 2, work all instep sts in established patt, beg and end with p2 (p1, p1, p2, p1); on Needle 3, k1, ssk, knit to end—2 gusset sts dec'd.

Rnd 3: On Needle 1 and Needle 3, knit; on Needle 2, work in established pattern.

Rep Rnds 2 and 3 until 40 (44, 48, 56, 60) sts rem—10 (10, 12, 15, 15) sts each on Needle 1 and Needle 3; 20 (24, 24, 26, 30) instep sts in rib patt on Needle 2.

Foot

Cont in established rib patt on instep sts and St st on other sts, work even until piece measures 5½ (6½, 7½, 8, 8¾)" (14 [16.5, 19, 20.5, 22] cm) from back of heel, or about 1½ (1¾, 2, 2¼, 2¼)" (3.8 [4.5, 5, 5.5, 5.5] cm) less than desired total foot length.

Toe

Rearrange sts if necessary so there are 10 (11, 12, 14, 15) sts each on Needle 1 and Needle 3, and 20 (22, 24, 28, 30) sts on Needle 2. Change to St st for all sts and work as foll:

Rnd 1: On Needle 1, knit to last 3 sts, k2tog, k1; on Needle 2, k1, ssk, work to last 3 sts, k2tog, k1; on Needle 3, k1, ssk, knit to end— 4 sts dec'd.

Rnd 2: Knit.

Rep Rnds 1 and 2 until 20 (20, 24, 28, 28) sts rem. Rep Rnd 1 *only* until 8 sts rem for all sizes. Knit sts from Needle 1 onto Needle 3, then re-arrange sts if necessary so there are 4 sts each on 2 needles for top and bottom of toe.

Finishing

Cut yarn, leaving an 18" (45.5 cm) tail. Using the Kitchener st (see pages 42–45), graft sts tog. Weave in loose ends. Block.

Spiral Rib Socks

The diagonal pattern on these thick socks is nothing more than a knit 2, purl 2 rib that shifts laterally 1 stitch every round. Because of this shift, the knit and purl stitches in the rib line up diagonally rather than vertically, and produce a flexible but non-binding leg. The pattern is identical on the two socks shown here, but if you want to make the socks mirror images of each other, simply shift the pattern one stitch to the left on one sock and one stitch to the right on the other.

These socks follow the basic pattern for 5 stitches per inch (see page 58) and are worked on four double-pointed needles.

Finished Size

About 6½ (7½, 8, 9, 9¾)" (16.5 [19, 20.5, 23, 25] cm) foot circumference and about 7 (8¼, 9½, 10¼, 11)" (18 [21, 24, 26, 28] cm) foot length from back of heel to tip of toe. To fit child medium (child large, adult small, adult medium, adult large); see page 51 for shoe size conversions. Socks shown measure 8" (20.5 cm) foot circumference.

Yarn

Worsted weight (#4 Medium; see page 12). *Shown here:* Brown Sheep Lamb's Pride Superwash Worsted (100% wool; 200 yd (183 m)/100 g): #SW197 cinnamon twist, 1 (1, 2, 2, 2) balls.

Needles

Upper leg—size 8 (5 mm): set of 4 double-pointed (dpn). Lower leg and foot—size 7 (4.5 mm): set of 4 dpn. Adjust needle size if necessary to obtain the correct gauge.

Notions

Marker (m); tapestry needle.

Gauge

10 stitches and 14 rounds = 2" (5 cm) in stockinette stitch worked in the round on smaller needles.

Stitch Guide

Spiral Rib (multiple of 4 sts)

Rnds 1 and 2: *K2, p2; rep from *.

Rnds 3 and 4: P1, *k2, p2; rep from * to last 3 sts, k2, p1.

Rnds 5 and 6: *P2, k2; rep from *.

Rnds 7 and 8: K1, *p2, k2; rep from * to last 3 sts, p2, k1.

Repeat Rnds 1–8 for pattern.

Leg

CO 32 (36, 40, 44, 48) sts. Place marker and join for working in rnds, being careful not to twist sts. Work in spiral rib (see Stitch Guide) until leg measures 5½ (6½, 7, 8, 8¾)" (14 [16.5, 18, 20.5, 22] cm) from CO, or desired length to top of heel.

Heel

K8 (9, 10, 11, 12), turn work around and with same needle, p16 (18, 20, 22, 24)—16 (18, 20, 22, 24) heel sts on one needle. Place rem 16 (18, 20, 22, 24) sts on spare needle(s) or holder to work later for instep.

Heel Flap

Work back and forth on heel sts in rows as foll:

Row 1: (RS) *Sl 1 pwise with yarn in back (wyb), k1; rep from *.

Row 2: Sl 1 pwise with yarn in front (wyf), purl to end.

Rep Rows 1 and 2 until a total of 16 (18, 20, 22, 24) rows have been worked—8 (9, 10, 11, 12) chain selvedge sts.

Turn Heel

Work short-rows as foll:

Row 1: (RS) K10 (11, 12, 13, 14), ssk, k1, turn work.

Row 2: (WS) Sl 1 pwise, p5, p2tog, p1, turn.

Row 3: Sl 1 pwise, knit to 1 st before gap made on previous row, ssk (1 st from each side of gap; see Glossary, page 133), k1, turn.

Row 4: Sl 1 pwise, purl to 1 st before gap made on previous row, p2tog (1 st from each side of gap), p1, turn.

Repeat Rows 3 and 4 until all heel sts have been worked, ending with a WS row and ending the last repeat as ssk on Row 3 and p2tog on Row 4 if there are not enough sts to work the final k1 or p1 after the dec—10 (12, 12, 14, 14) sts rem.

Gusset

Note: One extra st is picked up along the selvedge in the corner of each heel flap to avoid leaving a hole at the base of the gusset. Rejoin for working in the rnd as foll:

Rnd 1: With one needle (Needle 1), knit across all heel sts, then pick up and knit 9 (10, 11, 12, 13) sts along selvedge edge of heel flap; with another dpn (Needle 2), knit across 16 (18, 20, 22, 24) held instep sts; with another dpn (Needle 3), pick up and knit 9 (10, 11, 12, 13) sts along other side of heel flap, then knit across the first 5 (6, 6, 7, 7) heel sts from Needle 1 again—44 (50, 54, 60, 64) sts total; 14 (16, 17, 19, 20) sts each on Needle 1 and Needle 3; 16 (18, 20, 22, 24) instep sts on Needle 2. Rnd now begins at center back heel.

Rnd 2: On Needle 1, knit to last 3 sts, k2tog, k1; on Needle 2, knit across all instep sts; on Needle 3, k1, ssk, knit to end—2 gusset sts dec'd.

Rnd 3: Knit.

Rep Rnds 2 and 3 until 32 (36, 40, 44, 48) sts rem.

Foot

Work even in St st until piece measures 5½ (6½, 7½, 8, 8¾)" (14 [16.5, 19, 20.5, 22] cm) from back of heel, or about 1½ (1¾, 2, 2¼, 2¼)" (3.8 [4.5, 5, 5.5, 5.5] cm) less than desired total foot length.

Toe

Rnd 1: On Needle 1, knit to last 3 sts, k2tog, k1; on Needle 2, k1, ssk, knit to last 3 sts, k2tog, k1; on Needle 3, k1, ssk, knit to end—4 sts dec'd.

Rnd 2: Knit.

Rep Rnds 1 and 2 until 16 (16, 20, 20, 24) sts rem. Rep Rnd 1 *only* until 8 sts rem for all sizes. Knit sts from Needle 1 onto Needle 3—4 sts each on 2 needles.

Finishing

Cut yarn, leaving an 18" (45.5 cm) tail. Using the Kitchener st (see pages 42–45), graft sts tog. Weave in loose ends. Block.

Cable Patterns

Most cable patterns are based on a ribbed foundation, with the cable crosses worked on the columns of knit stitches bordered by purl stitches. This means that there are two factors causing the stitches to draw in: the juxtaposition of knit and purl stitches in the ribbed foundation and the crossed stitches in the cables. Therefore, you want to be sure to take accurate gauge measurements of the cable pattern before casting on for socks. To minimize draw-in contributed by cables, I generally choose cable patterns that involve just one- or two-stitch crosses, referred to as 1/1 or 2/2 cables.

The elongate nature of cables makes them attractive along the length of the leg and instep. However, be judicious about placing cables along the instep, where they could cause too much bulk in a shoe. You may find it more comfortable if the cable pattern ends at the ankle, and just the underlying rib continues along the instep. Or extend a single cable repeat along each side of the instep (called clocks, or clox), working the center stitches of the instep in rib.

Some of my favorite cable patterns for socks are shown here; check out books of stitch patterns (see Bibliography, page 135) for more choices.

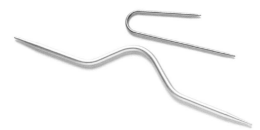

4-stitch repeats

Double Twists

7
5
3
1

Right Twist Lattice

15
13
11
9
7
5
3
1

	knit
•	purl
	RT: k2tog, then knit first st again
	LT: k second st tbl, knit first st
	2/2 RC: sl 2 sts onto cn and hold in back, k2, k2 from cn
	pattern repeat

6-stitch patterns

Double Twisted Rib

Staggered Twisted Rib

Spiral Rib

Flagon Stitch

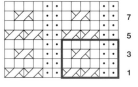

8-stitch patterns

Cable and Twist Rib

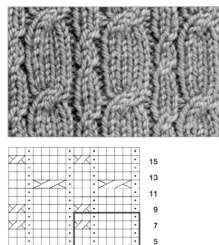

Elongated 6-Stitch Cable

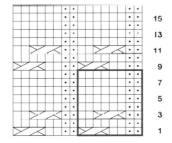

Twisted Rib

Staggered Baby Cables

Right-Twist Cable Rib Socks

In these socks, 1/1 cables travel across knit-4 ribs, giving the appearance of 2/2 cables without the draw-in. All of the cables cross in the same direction in these socks, but you could work all right-leaning crosses on one sock (as shown here) and all left-leaning crosses on the other. To prevent the crosses from adding unnecessary bulk and discomfort inside a shoe, the cables stop at the ankle.

These socks follow the basic pattern for 7 stitches per inch (see page 54) worked on four double-pointed needles, but the number of stitches cast-on and worked for the leg, heel, foot and toes for some of the sizes deviates from the basic pattern to accommodate the stitch pattern.

Finished Size

About 6½ (7½, 8, 9, 9¾)" (16.5 [19, 20.5, 23, 25] cm) foot circumference and about 7 (8¼, 9½, 10¼, 11)" (18 [21, 24, 26, 28] cm) foot length from back of heel to tip of toe. To fit child medium (child large, adult small, adult medium, adult large); see page 51 for shoe size conversions. Socks shown measure 8" (20.5 cm) foot circumference.

Yarn

Fingering weight (#1 Super Fine; see page 12). *Shown here:* Wooly West Footpath (85% wool, 15% nylon; 175 yd [160 m]/2 oz): yarrow, 2 (2, 2, 3, 3) skeins.

Needles

Upper leg—size 3 (3.25 mm). Lower leg and foot—size 2 (2.75 mm). Adjust needle size if necessary to obtain the correct gauge.

Notions

Markers (m); tapestry needle.

Gauge

14 stitches and 19 rounds = 2" (5 cm) in stockinette stitch worked in the round on smaller needles.

Stitch Guide

Right Twist (RT; worked over 2 sts)
K2tog but leave sts on needle, knit the first st again, slip both sts off needle.

Right-Twist Cable Rib (multiple of 7 sts)
Rnd 1: *K2, RT, p1, k1, p1; rep from *.
Rnd 2: *K1, RT, [k1, p1] 2 times; rep from *.
Rnd 3: *RT, k2, p1, k1, p1; rep from *.
Rnds 4–14: *K4, p1, k1, p1; rep from *.
Repeat Rnds 1–14 for pattern.

Leg

With larger needles and using the Old Norwegian method (see page 21), CO 42 (49, 56, 63, 70) sts. Place marker and join for working in rnds, being careful not to twist sts.

Cuff Pattern

*K4, p1, k1, p1; rep from * to end of rnd. Rep this rnd until piece measures 1½" (3.8 cm) from CO.

Leg Pattern

Work Rnds 1–14 of right twist cable rib patt (see Stitch Guide) until piece measures 2¾ (3¼, 3½, 4, 4½)" (7 [8.5, 9, 10, 11.5] cm) from CO. Change to smaller needles and cont in patt as established until piece measures about 5½ (6½, 7, 8, 8¾)" (14 [16.5, 18, 20.5, 22] cm) from CO, or desired length to top of heel, ending with Rnd 3 of patt.

Heel

K9 (8, 12, 18, 16), turn work around and with same needle, purl the next 21 (26, 27, 32, 35) sts and inc 1 (inc 0, inc 1, inc 0, dec 1) st as you go—22 (26, 28, 32, 34) heel sts on one needle. Place rem 21 (23, 29, 31, 35) sts on spare needle(s) or holder to work later for instep; the center st on instep needle should be k1 with a p1 on either side of it, and sts at each end of instep needle should be k2 (k3, k1, p1, k2).

Heel Flap

Work back and forth on heel sts in rows as foll:

Row 1: (RS) *Sl 1 pwise with yarn in back (wyb), k1; rep from *.

Row 2: Sl 1 pwise with yarn in front (wyf), purl to end.

Rep Rows 1 and 2 until a total of 22 (26, 28, 32, 34) rows have been worked—11 (13, 14, 16, 17) chain selvedge sts.

Turn Heel

Work short-rows as foll:

Row 1: (RS) K13 (15, 16, 18, 19), ssk, k1, turn work.

Row 2: (WS) Sl 1 pwise, p5, p2tog, p1, turn.

Row 3: Sl 1 pwise, knit to 1 st before gap made on previous row, ssk (1 st from each side of gap; see Glossary, page 133), k1, turn.

Row 4: Sl 1 pwise, purl to 1 st before gap made on previous row, p2tog (1 st from each side of gap), p1, turn.

Repeat Rows 3 and 4 until all heel sts have been worked, ending with a WS row and ending the last repeat as ssk on Row 3 and p2tog on Row 4 if there are not enough sts to work the final k1 or p1 after the dec—14 (16, 16, 18, 20) sts rem.

Gusset

Note: One extra st is picked up along the selvedge in the corner of each heel flap to avoid leaving a hole at the base of the gusset. Rejoin for working in the rnd as foll:

Rnd 1: With one needle (Needle 1), knit across all heel sts, then pick up and knit 12 (14, 15, 17, 18) sts along selvedge edge of heel flap; with another needle (Needle 2), work across 21 (23, 29, 31, 35) held instep sts working sts as they appear (knit the knits and purl the purls); with another needle (Needle 3), pick up and knit 12 (14, 15, 17, 18) sts along other side of heel flap, then knit across the first 7 (8, 8, 9, 10) heel sts from Needle 1 again—59 (67, 75, 83, 91) sts total; 19 (22, 23, 26, 28) sts each on Needle 1 and Needle 3; 21 (23, 29, 31, 35) instep sts on Needle 2. Rnd now begins at center back heel.

Rnd 2: On Needle 1, knit to last 3 sts, k2tog, k1; on Needle 2, work across instep sts as they appear; on Needle 3, k1, ssk, knit to end—2 gusset sts dec'd.

Rnd 3: On Needle 1 and Needle 3, knit; on Needle 2, work sts as they appear.

Rep Rnds 2 and 3 until 45 (53, 57, 65, 69) sts rem—12 (15, 14, 17, 17) sts each on Needle 1 and Needle 3; 21 (23, 29, 31, 35) instep sts on Needle 2. *Next rnd:* On Needle 1, knit to last 3 sts, k2tog, k1; on Needle 2, work sts as they appear; on Needle 3, knit to end—44 (52, 56, 64, 68) sts; 11 (14, 13, 16, 16) sts on Needle 1, 12 (15, 14, 17, 17) sts on Needle 3; 21 (23, 29, 31, 35) instep sts on Needle 2.

Foot

Work even in established patt until piece measures 5½ (6½, 7½, 8, 8¾)" (14 [16.5, 19, 20.5, 22] cm) from back of heel, or about 1½ (1¾, 2, 2¼, 2¼)" (3.8 [4.5, 5, 5.5, 5.5] cm) less than desired total foot length.

Toe

Rearrange sts so there are 11 (13, 14, 16, 17) sts each Needle 1 and Needle 3 and 22 (26, 28, 32, 34) sts on Needle 2. Work as foll:

Rnd 1: On Needle 1, knit to last 3 sts, k2tog, k1; on Needle 2, k1, ssk, knit to last 3 sts, k2tog, k1; on Needle 3, k1, ssk, knit to end—4 sts dec'd.

Rnd 2: Knit.

Rep Rnds 1 and 2 until 20 (24, 28, 32, 36) sts rem. Rep Rnd 1 *only* until 8 (8, 8, 12, 12) sts rem. Knit sts from Needle 1 onto Needle 3—4 (4, 4, 6, 6) sts each on 2 needles.

Finishing

Cut yarn, leaving an 18" (45.5 cm) tail. Using the Kitchener st (see pages 42–45), graft sts tog. Weave in loose ends. Block.

Cable Clock Socks

These socks show how just a little bit of cable can make an interesting design. One 2/2 cable panel is worked along each side of the leg and instep, and rather than crossing at equal intervals, the cable crosses alternate between every four and eight rows. The cables are separated by knit 2, purl 1 ribs, which help give the leg and foot a snug fit. For added interest, the ribs are worked into tiny 1/1 cables on the cuffs.

These socks follow the basic pattern for 8 stitches per inch (see page 52) worked on four double-pointed needles, but the number of stitches cast-on and worked for the leg, heel, foot and toes for some of the sizes deviates from the basic pattern to accommodate the stitch pattern.

Finished Size

About 6½ (7½, 8, 9, 9¾)" (16.5 [19, 20.5, 23, 25] cm) foot circumference and about 7 (8¼, 9½, 10¼, 11)" (18 [21, 24, 26, 28] cm) foot length from back of heel to tip of toe. To fit child medium (child large, adult small, adult medium, adult large); see page 51 for shoe size conversions. Socks shown measure 8" (20.5 cm) foot circumference.

Yarn

Fingering weight (#1 Super Fine; see page 12).
Shown here: Koigu Premium Merino (100% merino; 170 yd [155 m]/50 g): #2329 denim, 2 (2, 3, 3, 3) skeins.

Needles

Upper leg—size 3 (3.25 mm). Lower leg and foot—size 2 (2.75 mm). Adjust needle size if necessary to obtain the correct gauge.

Notions

Markers (m); cable needle; tapestry needle.

Gauge

16 stitches and 22 rounds = 2" (5 cm) in stockinette stitch worked in the round on smaller needles.

Stitch Guide

RT (worked over 2 sts)
K2tog but leave sts on needle, knit the first st again, slip both sts off needle.

2/2RC (worked over 4 sts)
Place 2 sts on cable needle and hold in back of work, k2, k2 from cable needle.

Leg

Cuff Pattern

With larger needles and using the Old Norwegian method (see page 21), CO 52 (61, 64, 73, 76) sts. Place marker and join for working in rnds, being careful not to twist sts.

Set-up rnd: [K2, p1] 4 (5, 5, 6, 6) times, k2, place marker (pm), p1, k4, p1, pm, [k2, p1] 4 (5, 6, 7, 8) times, k2, pm, p1, k4, p1, pm, [k2, p1] 4 (5, 5, 6, 6) times.

Odd-numbered Rnds 1–17: Work sts as they appear (knit the knits and purl the purls).

Rnds 2, 6, and 14: See Stitch Guide for RT and 2/2 RC definitions. [RT, p1] 4 (5, 5, 6, 6) times, RT, slip marker (sl m), p1, 2/2RC, p1, sl m, [RT, p1] 4 (5, 6, 7, 8) times, RT, sl m, p1, 2/2RC, p1, sl m, [RT, p1] 4 (5, 5, 6, 6) times.

Rnds 4, 8, 12, and 16: Work sts as they appear.

Rnd 10: [RT, p1] 4 (5, 5, 6, 6) times, RT, sl m, p1, k4, p1, sl m, [RT, p1] 4 (5, 6, 7, 8) times, RT, sl m, p1, k4, p1, sl m, [RT, p1] 4 (5, 5, 6, 6) times.

Rnd 18: [RT, p1] 4 (5, 5, 6, 6) times, RT, sl m, p1, 2/2RC, p1, sl m, [RT, p1] 4 (5, 6, 7, 8) times, RT, sl m, p1, 2/2RC, p1, sl m, [RT, p1] 4 (5, 5, 6, 6) times—piece measures about 1½" (3.8 cm) from CO.

Leg Pattern

Working the 2-st RT columns as k2 throughout, cont in patt for leg as foll:

Rnds 1–7: Work sts as they appear.

Rnd 8: [K2, p1] 4 (5, 5, 6, 6) times, k2, sl m, p1, 2/2RC, p1, sl m, [k2, p1] 4 (5, 6, 7, 8) times, k2, sl m, p1, 2/2RC, p1, sl m, [k2, p1] 4 (5, 5, 6, 6) times.

Rnds 9–11: Work sts as they appear.

Rnd 12: Rep Rnd 8.

Rep Rnds 1–12 for patt, changing to smaller needles when leg measures 2¾ (3¼, 3½, 4, 4½)" (7 [8.5, 9, 10, 11.5] cm) from CO. Cont in patt until leg measures about 5½ (6½, 7, 8, 8¾)" (14 [16.5, 18, 20.5, 22] cm) from CO, or desired length to top of heel, and end having just completed cable crossing Rnd 8 or 12 of patt.

Heel

K14 (17, 17, 20, 20), turn work around and with same needle, sl 1, 25 (31, 31, 37, 37)—26 (32, 32, 38, 38) heel sts on one needle. Place rem 26 (29, 32, 35, 38) sts on spare needle(s) or holder to work later for instep; sts at each end of instep needle should be the 6 sts of cable patt (p1, k4, p1).

Heel Flap

Work back and forth on heel sts in rows as foll:

Row 1: (RS) *Sl 1 pwise with yarn in back (wyb), k1; rep from *.

Row 2: Sl 1 pwise with yarn in front (wyf), purl to end.

Rep Rows 1 and 2 until a total of 26 (30, 32, 36, 38) rows have been worked—13 (15, 16, 18, 19) chain selvedge sts.

Turn Heel

Work short-rows as foll:

Row 1: (RS) K15 (18, 18, 21, 21), ssk, k1, turn work.

Row 2: (WS) Sl 1 pwise, p5, p2tog, p1, turn.

Row 3: Sl 1 pwise, knit to 1 st before gap made on previous row, ssk (1 st from each side of gap; see Glossary, page 133), k1, turn.

Row 4: Sl 1 pwise, purl to 1 st before gap made on previous row, p2tog (1 st from each side of gap), p1, turn.

Repeat Rows 3 and 4 until all heel sts have been worked, ending with a WS row and ending the last repeat ssk on Row 3 and p2tog on Row 4 if there are not enough sts to work the final k1 or p1 after the dec—16 (18, 18, 22, 22) sts rem.

Gusset

Note: One extra st is picked up along the selvedge in the corner of each heel flap to avoid leaving a hole at the base of the gusset. Rejoin for working in the rnd as foll:

Rnd 1: With one needle (Needle 1), knit across all heel sts, then pick up and knit 14 (16, 17, 19, 20) sts along selvedge edge of heel flap; with another needle (Needle 2), work across 26 (29, 32, 35, 38) held instep sts in established patt (beg and end with 6-st cable patt); with another needle (Needle 3), pick up and knit 14 (16, 17, 19, 20) sts along other side of heel flap, then knit across the first 8 (9, 9, 11, 11) heel sts from Needle 1 again—70 (79, 84, 95, 100) sts total; 22 (25, 26, 30, 31) sts each on Needle 1 and Needle 3; 26 (29, 32, 35, 38) instep sts on Needle 2. Rnd now begins at center back heel.

Rnd 2: On Needle 1, knit to last 3 sts, k2tog, k1; on Needle 2, work across instep sts in established patt; on Needle 3, k1, ssk, knit to end—2 gusset sts dec'd.

Rnd 3: On Needle 1 and Needle 3, knit; on Needle 2, work in patt, crossing cables at established intervals.

Rep Rnds 2 and 3 until 52 (61, 64, 73, 76) sts rem—13 (16, 16, 19, 19) sts each on Needle 1 and Needle 3; 26 (29, 32, 35, 38) instep sts on Needle 2.

Foot

Work even in established patt until piece measures 5½ (6½, 7½, 8, 8¾)" (14 [16.5, 19, 20.5, 22] cm) from back of heel, or about 1½ (1¾, 2, 2¼, 2¼)" (3.8 [4.5, 5, 5.5, 5.5] cm) less than desired total foot length, and end having just completed cable crossing Rnd 8 or 12 of patt.

Toe

Knit 1 rnd on all sts, dec 0 (1, 0, 1, 0) st on instep needle—52 (60, 64, 72, 76) sts. Rearrange sts if necessary so there are 13 (15, 16, 18, 19) sts each Needle 1 and Needle 3 and 26 (30, 32, 36, 38) sts on Needle 2. Work as foll:

Rnd 1: On Needle 1, knit to last 3 sts, k2tog, k1; on Needle 2, k1, ssk, knit to last 3 sts, k2tog, k1; on Needle 3, k1, ssk, knit to end—4 sts dec'd.

Rnd 2. Knit.

Rep Rnds 1 and 2 until 24 (28, 32, 36, 40) sts rem. Rep Rnd 1 *only* until 8 (8, 12, 12, 16) sts rem. Knit sts from Needle 1 onto Needle 3—4 (4, 6, 6, 8) sts each on 2 needles.

Finishing

Cut yarn, leaving an 18" (45.5 cm) tail. Using the Kitchener st (see pages 42–45), graft sts tog. Weave in loose ends. Block.

Lace Patterns

Lace patterns can transform the common sock into a fancy or feminine accessory. However, not all lace patterns are suitable for socks. The openwork designs characteristic of some lace patterns have very little elasticity, making a fabric that falls to your ankle instead of hugging your leg. Be sure to measure your gauge on the lace pattern before you cast on stitches for a sock.

It's a good idea to use lace patterns that incorporate some rib components, such as 1 or 2 purl stitches or knit 1, purl 1 rib stitches between lace panels, or work lace patterns with yarns that contain a bit of elastic to compensate for the tendency of the pattern to stretch. Lace patterns look nice as accent patterns on the cuffs, as allover patterns along the leg (and instep), and as single panels along the sides of the leg or instep. Take advantage of the scalloped cast-on edges of some lace patterns to add a pretty edge at the top of the leg.

Some of my favorite lace patterns for socks are shown here; check out books of stitch patterns (see Bibliography, page 135) for other ideas.

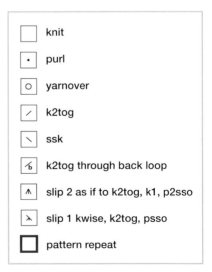

☐	knit
·	purl
○	yarnover
╱	k2tog
╲	ssk
⋌	k2tog through back loop
⋀	slip 2 as if to k2tog, k1, p2sso
⋏	slip 1 kwise, k2tog, psso
☐	pattern repeat

4-stitch repeats

Stockinette Ladder Lace

Right-Twist Lace Rib

Simple Lace Rib

Wide Lace Rib

6-stitch repeats

Little Arrowhead

	O	∧	O			O	∧	O				7
O	/			＼	O	O	/			＼	O	5
	O	∧	O			O	∧	O				3
O	/			＼	O	O	/			＼	O	1

Lacy Zigzag

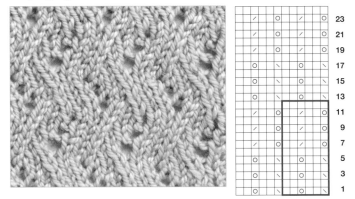

	/		O		/		O	23
	/		O		/		O	21
	/		O		/		O	19
	O		＼		O		＼	17
	O		＼		O		＼	15
	O		＼		O		＼	13
	/		O		/		O	11
	/		O		/		O	9
	/		O		/		O	7
	O		＼		O		＼	5
	O		＼		O		＼	3
	O		＼		O		＼	1

Double Lace Rib

•		O	/	•		•		O	/	•		7
•			•		•			•		5
•	⁄b	O	•		•	⁄b	O	•		5
•		O	/	•		•		O	/	•		3
•			•		•			•		
•	⁄b	O	•		•	⁄b	O	•		1

Clover Leaf Eyelet Rib

•				•				•			11
•				•				•			
•	＼	O		•		＼	O	•		9
•				•				•			
•	O	∧	O	•	O	∧	O	•		7
•				•				•			5
•	＼	O		•		＼	O	•		3
•				•				•			
•	O	∧	O	•	O	∧	O	•		1

See page 84 for symbol key.

8-stitch repeats

Faggoting Ribs

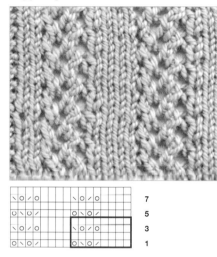

```
\ O / O      \ O / O         7
O \ O /      O \ O /         5
\ O / O      \ O / O         3
O \ O /      O \ O /         1
```

Little Bells

```
O λ O    O λ O    O λ O    O λ O    15
   O λ O       O λ O          13
O λ O         O λ O           11
O λ O         O λ O            9
O λ O    O λ O    O λ O    O λ O    7
   O λ O       O λ O           5
O λ O         O λ O            3
O λ O         O λ O            1
```

Left-Slant Wishbone

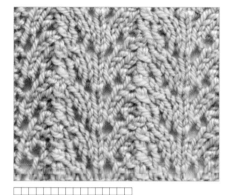

```
   O λ O         O λ O       11
O     λ     O   O     λ     O   9
O       λ       O  O       λ       O   7
   O λ O         O λ O        5
O     λ     O   O     λ     O   3
O       λ       O  O       λ       O   1
```

Centered Wishbone

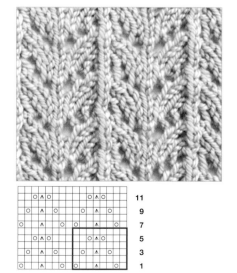

```
   O ∧ O         O ∧ O       11
O     ∧     O   O     ∧     O   9
O       ∧       O  O       ∧       O   7
   O ∧ O         O ∧ O        5
O     ∧     O   O     ∧     O   3
O       ∧       O  O       ∧       O   1
```

Herringbone Lace Socks

These comfortable socks are worked with a relatively simple 6-stitch lace pattern around the leg and along the instep. The pattern begins on the very first row after the stitches are cast on, which forms pretty scallops along the top edge. Normally, this lace pattern would have very little stretch because there are no ribbed stitches incorporated into the repeats. But because the yarn contains some elastic, the stitches have plenty of stretch and resilience, even without ribs.

These socks follow the basic pattern for 6 stitches per inch (see page 56) worked on four double-pointed needles, but the leg is shorter for a dressier look.

Finished Size

About 6½ (7½, 8, 9, 9¾)" (16.5 [19, 20.5, 23, 25] cm) foot circumference and about 7 (8¼, 9½, 10¼, 11)" (18 [21, 24, 26, 28] cm) foot length from back of heel to tip of toe. To fit child medium (child large, adult small, adult medium, adult large); see page 51 for shoe size conversions. Socks shown measure 8" (20.5 cm) foot circumference.

Yarn

Sportweight (#2 Fine; see page 12).
Shown here: Cascade Fixation (98.3% cotton, 1.7% elastic; 100 yd [90 m]/50 g): #2406 lavender, 2 (2, 2, 3, 3) balls.

Needles

Size 5 (3.75 mm): set of 4 double-pointed (dpn). Adjust needle size if necessary to obtain the correct gauge.

Notions

Marker (m); tapestry needle.

Gauge

12 stitches and 22 rounds = 2" (5 cm) in stockinette stitch worked in the round.

Stitch Guide

Herringbone Lace (multiple of 6 sts)

Rnds 1, 3, 5, 7, 9, and 11: Knit.
Rnds 2, 4, and 6: *Ssk, k2, yo, k2; rep from *.
Rnds 8, 10, and 12: *K2, yo, k2, k2tog; rep from *.
Repeat Rnds 1–12 for pattern.

Leg

Using the Old Norwegian method (see page 21), CO 42 (42, 48, 54, 60) sts. Place marker and join for working in rnds, being careful not to twist sts. Work Rnds 1–12 of herringbone lace (see Stitch Guide) 4 (5, 5, 6, 6) times—piece measures about 4 (5, 5, 6, 6)" (10 [12.5, 12.5, 15, 15] cm) from CO with top edge unrolled.

Heel

K11 (11, 9, 11, 15), turn work around and with same needle, p22 (22, 24, 28, 30)—22 (22, 24, 28, 30) heel sts on one needle. Place rem 20 (20, 24, 26, 30) sts on spare needle(s) or holder to work later for instep. *Note:* The 18 (18, 18, 24, 24) center sts on instep needle should be 3 (3, 3, 4, 4) complete 6-st reps of lace patt; the 1 (1, 3, 1, 3) st(s) on either side of center sts will be worked later in St st.

Heel Flap

Work back and forth on heel sts in rows as foll:

Row 1: (RS) *Sl 1 pwise with yarn in back (wyb), k1; rep from *.

Row 2: Sl 1 pwise with yarn in front (wyf), purl to end.

Rep Rows 1 and 2 until a total of 20 (22, 24, 26, 28) rows have been worked—10 (11, 12, 13, 14) chain selvedge sts.

Turn Heel

Work short-rows as foll:

Row 1: (RS) K13 (13, 14, 16, 17), ssk, k1, turn work.

Row 2: (WS) Sl 1 pwise, p5, p2tog, p1, turn.

Row 3: Sl 1 pwise, knit to 1 st before gap made on previous row, ssk (1 st from each side of gap; see Glossary, page 133), k1, turn.

Row 4: Sl 1 pwise, purl to 1 st before gap made on previous row, p2tog (1 st from each side of gap), p1, turn.

Repeat Rows 3 and 4 until all heel sts have been worked, ending with a WS row and ending the last repeat as ssk on Row 3 and p2tog on Row 4 if there are not enough sts to work the final k1 or p1 after the dec—14 (14, 14, 16, 18) sts rem.

Gusset

Note: One extra st is picked up along the selvedge in the corner of each heel flap to avoid leaving a hole at the base of the gusset. Rejoin for working in the rnd as foll:

Rnd 1: With one needle (Needle 1), knit across all heel sts, then pick up and knit 11 (12, 13, 14, 15) sts along selvedge edge of heel flap; with another dpn (Needle 2), work across held instep sts as k1 (1, 3, 1, 3), work center 18 (18, 18, 24, 24) sts in established lace patt, k1 (1, 3, 1, 3); with another dpn (Needle 3), pick up and knit 11 (12, 13, 14, 15) sts along other side of heel flap, then knit across the first 7 (7,

7, 8, 9) heel sts from Needle 1 again—56 (58, 64, 70, 78) sts total; 18 (19, 20, 22, 24) sts each on Needle 1 and Needle 3; 20 (20, 24, 26, 30) instep sts on Needle 2. Rnd now begins at center back heel.

Rnd 2: On Needle 1, knit to last 3 sts, k2tog, k1; on Needle 2, work instep sts in patt as established with St sts at each side; on Needle 3, k1, ssk, knit to end—2 gusset sts dec'd.

Rnd 3: Work even in established patts.

Rep Rnds 2 and 3 until 40 (44, 48, 52, 56) sts rem—10 (12, 12, 13, 13) sts each on Needle 1 and Needle 3; 20 (20, 24, 26, 30) instep sts on Needle 2.

Foot

Cont in patt as established until piece measures 5½ (6½, 7½, 8, 8¾)" (14 [16.5, 19, 20.5, 22] cm) from back of heel, or about 1½ (1¾, 2, 2¼, 2¼)" (3.8 [4.5, 5, 5.5, 5.5] cm) less than desired total foot length, ending with Rnd 6 or 12 of lace patt.

Toe

Rearrange sts if necessary so there are 10 (11, 12, 13, 14) sts each on Needle 1 and Needle 3, and 20 (22, 24, 26, 28) sts on Needle 2. Change to St st for all sts, and work as foll:

Rnd 1: On Needle 1, knit to last 3 sts, k2tog, k1; on Needle 2, k1, ssk, knit to last 3 sts, k2tog, k1; on Needle 3, k1, ssk, knit to end—4 sts dec'd.

Rnd 2: Knit.

Rep Rnds 1 and 2 until 20 (20, 24, 28, 28) sts rem. Rep Rnd 1 only until 8 sts rem for all sizes. Knit sts from Needle 1 onto Needle 3—4 sts each on 2 needles.

Finishing

Cut yarn, leaving an 18" (45.5 cm) tail. Using the Kitchener st (see pages 42–45), graft sts tog. Weave in loose ends. Block.

Chevron Lace Socks

A simple 7-stitch chevron pattern forms tiny zigs and zags around the legs and down the sides of the insteps of these colorful socks. Although there are no rib stitches between the pattern repeats, the juxtaposition of left-leaning and right-leaning decreases creates a boundary that behaves much like a purl stitch between pattern repeats. In many cases, space-dyed yarns obscure stitch patterns, but here the color changes help to define the peaks and valleys of the chevrons.

These socks follow the basic pattern for 7 stitches per inch (see page 54) worked on four double-pointed needles, but the stitch count is adjusted for some sizes to accommodate full pattern repeats and the leg is worked for fewer rounds for a dressier look.

Finished Size

About 6½ (7½, 8, 9, 9¾)" (16.5 [19, 20.5, 23, 25] cm) foot circumference and about 7 (8¼, 9½, 10¼, 11)" (18 [21, 24, 26, 28] cm) foot length from back of heel to tip of toe. To fit child medium (child large, adult small, adult medium, adult large); see page 51 for shoe size conversions. Socks shown measure 8" (20.5 cm) foot circumference.

Yarn

Fingering weight (#1 Super Fine; see page 12). *Shown here:* Lorna's Laces Shepherd Sock Multi (80% superwash wool, 20% nylon; 215 yd [196 m]/2 oz [56.7 g]): #74 mother lode, 2 (2, 2, 2, 3) skeins.

Needles

Size 3 (3.25 mm): set of 4 double-pointed (dpn). Adjust needle size if necessary to obtain the correct gauge.

Notions

Marker (m); tapestry needle.

Gauge

14 stitches and 20 rounds = 2" (5 cm) in stock-inette stitch worked in the round.

Stitch Guide

Chevron Lace Pattern (multiple of 7 sts)

Rnd 1: Knit.

Rnd 2: *K2tog, k1, knit into back of st below first st on left needle, knit first st on left needle, knit into back of same st below needle again (3 sts worked in 1 st), k1, ssk; rep from *.

Repeat Rnds 1–2 for pattern.

Leg

Using the Old Norwegian method (see page 21), CO 42 (49, 56, 63, 70) sts. Place marker and join for working in rnds, being careful not to twist sts. Work Rnds 1 and 2 of chevron lace patt (see Stitch Guide) until piece measures 4 (4½, 5, 6, 6½)" (10 [11.5, 12.5, 15, 16.5] cm) from CO.

Heel

K21 (25, 28, 33, 35) and inc 2 (inc 3, inc 0, inc 1, dec 1) st(s) evenly spaced as you go, turn work around and with same needle, p22 (26, 28, 32, 34)—22 (26, 28, 32, 34) heel sts on one needle. Place rem 22 (26, 28, 32, 35) sts on spare needle (s) or holder to work later for in-step.

Heel Flap

Work back and forth on heel sts in rows as foll:

Row 1: (RS) *Sl 1 pwise with yarn in back (wyb), k1; rep from *.

Row 2: Sl 1 pwise with yarn in front (wyf), purl to end.

Rep Rows 1 and 2 until a total of 22 (26, 28, 32, 34) rows have been worked—11 (13, 14, 16, 17) chain selvedge sts.

Turn Heel

Work short-rows as foll:

Row 1: (RS) K13 (15, 16, 18, 19), ssk, k1, turn work.

Row 2: (WS) Sl 1 pwise, p5, p2tog, p1, turn.

Row 3: Sl 1 pwise, knit to 1 st before gap made on previous row, ssk (1 st from each side of gap, k1, turn.

Row 4: Sl 1 pwise, purl to 1 st before gap made on previous row, p2tog (1 st from each side of gap), p1, turn.

Repeat Rows 3 and 4 until all heel sts have been worked, ending with a WS row and ending the last repeat ssk on Row 3 and p2tog on Row 4 if there are not enough sts to work the final k1 or p1 after the dec—14 (16, 16, 18, 20) sts rem.

Gusset

Note: One extra st is picked up along the selvedge in the corner of each heel flap to avoid leaving a hole at the base of the gusset. Rejoin for working in the rnd as foll:

Rnd 1: With one needle (Needle 1), knit across all heel sts, then pick up and knit 12 (14, 15, 17, 18) sts along selvedge edge of heel flap; with another dpn (Needle 2), work across held in-step sts as k0 (3, 0, 2, 0), work 7 sts in estab-lished lace patt, k7 (7, 14, 14, 21) and dec 0 (0, 0, 0, 1) st as you go, work 7 sts in estab-lished lace patt, k1 (2, 0, 2, 0); with another dpn (Needle 3), pick up and knit 12 (14, 15, 17, 18) sts along other side of heel flap, then knit across the first 7 (8, 8, 9, 10) heel sts from Needle 1 again—60 (70, 74, 84, 90) sts total; 19 (22, 23, 26, 28) sts each on Needle 1 and Needle 3; 22 (26, 28, 32, 34) instep sts on Needle 2. Rnd now begins at center back heel.

Rnd 2: On Needle 1, knit to last 3 sts, k2tog, k1; on Needle 2, k0 (3, 0, 2, 0), work 7 sts in established patt, k7 (7, 14, 14, 20), work 7 sts in established patt, k1 (2, 0, 2, 0); on Needle 3, k1, ssk, knit to end—2 gusset sts dec'd.

Rnd 3: Work even as established.

Rep Rnds 2 and 3 until 44 (52, 56, 64, 68) sts rem—11 (13, 14, 16, 17) sts each on Needle 1 and Needle 3; 22 (26, 28, 32, 34) instep sts on Needle 2.

Foot

Work even until piece measures 5½ (6½, 7½, 8, 8¾)" (14 [16.5, 19, 20.5, 22] cm) from back of heel, or about 1½ (1¾, 2, 2¼, 2¼)" (3.8 [4.5, 5, 5.5, 5.5] cm) less than desired total foot length.

Toe

Rnd 1: On Needle 1, knit to last 3 sts, k2tog, k1; on Needle 2, k1, ssk, knit to last 3 sts, k2tog, k1; on Needle 3, k1, ssk, knit to end—4 sts dec'd.

Rnd 2: Knit.

Rep Rnds 1 and 2 until 20 (24, 28, 32, 36) sts rem. Rep Rnd 1 *only* until 8 (8, 8, 12, 12) sts rem. Knit sts from Needle 1 onto Needle 3— 4 (4, 4, 6, 6) sts each on 2 needles.

Finishing

Cut yarn, leaving an 18" (45.5 cm) tail. Using the Kitchener st (see pages 42–45), graft sts tog. Weave in loose ends. Block.

6
Cuff and Leg Variations

So far, all of the sock patterns in this book have had a crew shape with legs that begin about halfway down the calf. But it's a small matter to change the length or look of the cuff or leg. You can make anklets by working fewer rows to the beginning of the heel or knee socks by working more rows. You can make cuffs more decorative with ruffled edges or picot hems.

The following projects are just a few of the ways you can change the basic pattern. Any of these variations can be applied to any other project in this book. For example, translate the Picot Anklets (page 122) into a dressy crew by adding a picot hem at the cuff and working the leg the normal length in stockinette stitch or add a fold-over ruffle cuff to make a lace sock even fancier. Try extending the leg of any sock into a knee-high.

To make a knee-high fit comfortably, you'll need to add width for the calf. The best way to do this is to add stitches to the upper leg. To determine how much wider to make the calf, measure the circumference of your leg at the widest part of your calf, then subtract the foot circumference (which conveniently corresponds to the standard leg circumference) from this measurement. Using your gauge as a guide, translate this number of inches into a number of stitches. This is the number of extra stitches to cast on for the upper leg and the number of stitches you'll want to decrease as you work down past the calf.

If this seems like too much trouble, you can simply use different needle sizes to control the circumference through your gauge. For example, cast on with needles two or three sizes larger than needed to get gauge, then change to progressively smaller needles as you work down the leg, past the calf muscle. Of course, it's prudent to try on the piece as you go to make sure that size is right. It's also a good idea to work the leg in a stitch pattern that contains an element of ribs that will provide some elasticity for a snug and flexible fit.

Picot Anklets

These anklets are a lot like short sport socks; they're even knitted with comfortable, breathable cotton yarn. The double-thickness cuff begins with a facing, followed by a fold line worked in a picot stitch, and ends with the part that is visible on the outside. After the socks are knitted, the facing is turned to the inside along the picot row and sewn in place. The fold line forms a decorative edge punctuated with tiny scallops. Because the yarn contains elastic, the socks have plenty of stretch and hug, even without ribs.

The instructions here are modified from the basic sock pattern for 6 stitches to the inch (see page 56) worked on four double-pointed needles.

Finished Size

About 6½ (7½, 8, 9, 9¾)" (16.5 [19, 20.5, 23, 25] cm) foot circumference and about 7 (8¼, 9½, 10¼, 11)" (18 [21, 24, 26, 28] cm) foot length from back of heel to tip of toe. To fit child medium (child large, adult small, adult medium, adult large); see page 51 for shoe size conversions. Socks shown measure 7½" (19 cm) foot circumference.

Yarn

Sportweight (#2 Fine; see page 12).
Shown here: Cascade Fixation (98.3% cotton, 1.7% elastic; 100 yd [90 m]/50 g): #3794 burgundy, 2 (2, 2, 2, 3) balls

Needles

Size 5 (3.75 mm): set of 4 double-pointed (dpn). Adjust needle size if necessary to obtain the correct gauge.

Notions

Marker (m); tapestry needle.

Gauge

12 stitches and 22 rounds = 2" (5 cm) in stockinette stitch worked in the round.

Leg

Loosely CO 40 (44, 48, 52, 56) sts. Place marker and join for working in rnds, being careful not to twist sts. Work even in St st until piece measures 2" (5 cm) from CO. *Picot fold line:* *K2tog, yo; rep from * to end of rnd. Work even in St st until piece measures 2½" (6.5 cm) from fold line.

Heel

K10 (11, 12, 13, 14), turn work around and with same needle, p20 (22, 24, 26, 28)—20 (22, 24, 26, 28) heel sts on one needle. Place rem 20 (22, 24, 26, 28) sts on spare needle(s) or holder to work later for instep.

Heel Flap

Work back and forth on heel sts in rows as foll:

Row 1: (RS) *Sl 1 pwise with yarn in back (wyb), k1; rep from *.

Row 2: Sl 1 pwise with yarn in front (wyf), purl to end.

Rep Rows 1 and 2 until a total of 20 (22, 24, 26, 28) rows have been worked—10 (11, 12, 13, 14) chain selvedge sts.

Turn Heel

Work short-rows as foll:

Row 1: (RS) K12 (13, 14, 15, 16), ssk, k1, turn work.

Row 2: (WS) Sl 1 pwise, p5, p2tog, p1, turn.

Row 3: Sl 1 pwise, knit to 1 st before gap made on previous row, ssk (1 st from each side of gap; see Glossary, page 133), k1, turn.

Row 4: Sl 1 pwise, purl to 1 st before gap made on previous row, p2tog (1 st from each side of gap), p1, turn.

Repeat Rows 3 and 4 until all heel sts have been worked, ending with a WS row and ending the last repeat as ssk on Row 3 and p2tog on Row 4 if there are not enough sts to work the final k1 or p1 after the dec—12 (14, 14, 16, 16) sts rem.

Gusset

Note: One extra st is picked up along the selvedge in the corner of each heel flap to avoid leaving a hole at the base of the gusset. Rejoin for working in the rnd as foll:

Rnd 1: With one needle (Needle 1), knit across all heel sts, then pick up and knit 11 (12, 13, 14, 15) sts along selvedge edge of heel flap; with another dpn (Needle 2), work across 20 (22, 24, 26, 28) held instep sts; with another dpn (Needle 3), pick up and knit 11 (12, 13, 14, 15) sts along other side of heel flap, then knit across the first 6 (7, 7, 8, 8) heel sts from Needle 1 again—54 (60, 64, 70, 74) sts total; 17 (19, 20, 22, 23) sts each on Needle 1 and Needle 3; 20 (22, 24, 26, 28) instep sts on Needle 2. Rnd now begins at center back heel.

Rnd 2: On Needle 1, knit to last 3 sts, k2tog, k1; on Needle 2, knit across all instep sts; on Needle 3, k1, ssk, knit to end—2 gusset sts dec'd.

Rnd 3: Knit.

Rep Rnds 2 and 3 until 40 (44, 48, 52, 56) sts rem—10 (11, 12, 13, 14) sts each on Needle 1 and Needle 3; 20 (22, 24, 26, 28) instep sts on Needle 2.

Foot

Work even until piece measures 5½ (6½, 7½, 8, 8¾)" (14 [16.5, 19, 20.5, 22] cm) from back of heel, or about 1½ (1¾, 2, 2¼, 2¼)" (3.8 [4.5, 5, 5.5, 5.5] cm) less than desired total foot length.

Toe

Rnd 1: On Needle 1, knit to last 3 sts, k2tog, k1; on Needle 2, k1, ssk, work to last 3 sts, k2tog, k1; on Needle 3, k1, ssk, knit to end—4 sts dec'd.

Rnd 2: Knit.

Rep Rnds 1 and 2 until 20 (20, 24, 28, 28) sts rem. Rep Rnd 1 *only* until 8 sts rem for all sizes. Knit sts from Needle 1 onto Needle 3—4 sts each on 2 needles.

Finishing

Cut yarn, leaving an 18" (45.5 cm) tail. Using the Kitchener st (see pages 42–45), graft sts tog. Fold top 2" (5 cm) of sock to inside along picot fold line for cuff facing. With yarn threaded on a tapestry needle, sew cuff facing to WS of cuff about 4 rows above beg of heel shaping. Weave in loose ends. Block.

Ruffle Cuff Anklets

These pretty socks are fashioned after those typically reserved for little girls. But why should they have all the fun? The socks begin at the wide edge of the ribbed ruffle. To shape the ruffle, stitches are decreased every few rounds to turn a knit 5, purl 2 rib into a knit 4, purl 2 rib, then into a knit 3, purl 2 rib, and finally into a knit 3, purl 1 rib. The work is reversed at the top of the ruffle so that the wrong side of the ruffle corresponds to the right side of the sock, and a snug knit 1 purl 1 rib is worked for the length of the ruffle to hold the cuff in place. The rest of the sock is worked in stockinette stitch.

The instructions here are modified from the basic sock pattern for 8 stitches to the inch (see page 52) worked on four double-pointed needles.

Finished Size

About 6½ (7½, 8, 9, 9¾)" (16.5 [19, 20.5, 23, 25] cm) foot circumference and about 7 (8¼, 9½, 10¼, 11)" (18 [21, 24, 26, 28] cm) foot length from back of heel to tip of toe. To fit child medium (child large, adult small, adult medium, adult large); see page 51 for shoe size conversions. Anklets shown measure 7½" (19 cm) foot length.

Yarn

Fingering weight (#2 Fine; see page 12).
Shown here: Louet Gems Fingering Weight (100% merino wool; 185 yd [169 m]/50 g): #48 aqua, 2 (2, 2, 3, 3) skeins.

Needles

Size 2 (2.75 mm): set of 4 double-pointed (dpn). Adjust needle size if necessary to obtain the correct gauge.

Notions

Marker (m); tapestry needle.

Gauge

16 stitches and 20 rounds = 2" (5 cm) in stockinette stitch worked in the round.

Leg

Using the Old Norwegian method (see page 21), CO 91 (105, 112, 126, 133) sts. Place marker and join for working in rnds, being careful not to twist sts. Work ruffle rib patt as foll:

Rnds 1–6: *K5, p2; rep from *.

Rnd 7: (dec rnd) *K3, k2tog, p2; rep from *—78 (90, 96, 108, 114) sts rem.

Rnds 8–12: *K4, p2; rep from *.

Rnd 13: (dec rnd) *Ssk (see Glossary, page 133), k2, p2; rep from *—65 (75, 80, 90, 95) sts rem.

Rnds 14–18: *K3, p2; rep from *.

Rnd 19: (dec rnd) *K3, p2tog; rep from *—52 (60, 64, 72, 76) sts rem.

Rnds 20–24: *K3, p1; rep from *—piece measures about 2½" (6.5 cm) from CO.

Fold line: Push work through the center of the needles so the WS is facing, and knit all sts for 1 rnd to form fold line. *Note:* The WS of ribbed cuff corresponds to the RS of the rest of the sock; the RS of cuff will show on outside of sock when cuff is folded down. *Next rnd:* (RS of sock; WS of cuff) *K1, p1; rep from *. Cont in k1, p1 rib for 23 more rnds—piece measures about 2½" (6.5 cm) from fold line. Change to St st and work 10 rnds even—piece measures about 6" (15 cm) from CO and 3½" (9 cm) from fold line.

Heel

K13 (15, 16, 18, 19), turn work around and with same needle, p26 (30, 32, 36, 38)—26 (30, 32, 36, 38) heel sts on one needle. Place rem 26 (30, 32, 36, 38) sts on spare needle(s) or holder to work later for instep.

Heel Flap

Work back and forth on heel sts in rows as foll:

Row 1: (RS) *Sl 1 pwise with yarn in back (wyb), k1; rep from *.

Row 2: Sl 1 pwise with yarn in front (wyf), purl to end.

Rep Rows 1 and 2 until a total of 26 (30, 32, 36, 38) rows have been worked—13 (15, 16, 18, 19) chain selvedge sts.

Turn Heel

Work short-rows as foll:

Row 1: (RS) K15 (17, 18, 20, 21), ssk, k1, turn work.

Row 2: (WS) Sl 1 pwise, p5, p2tog, p1, turn.

Row 3: Sl 1 pwise, knit to 1 st before gap made on previous row, ssk (1 st from each side of gap), k1, turn.

Row 4: Sl 1 pwise, purl to 1 st before gap made on previous row, p2tog (1 st from each side of gap), p1, turn.

Repeat Rows 3 and 4 until all heel sts have been worked, ending with a WS row and ending the last repeat ssk on Row 3 and p2tog on Row 4 if there are not enough sts to work the final k1 or p1 after the dec—16 (18, 18, 20, 22) sts rem.

Gusset

Note: One extra st is picked up along the selvedge in the corner of each heel flap to avoid leaving a hole at the base of the gusset. Rejoin for working in the rnd as foll:

Rnd 1: With one needle (Needle 1), knit across all heel sts, then pick up and knit 14 (16, 17, 19, 20) sts along selvedge edge of heel flap; with another needle (Needle 2), work across 26 (30, 32, 36, 38) held instep sts; with another needle (Needle 3), pick up and knit 14 (16, 17, 19, 20) sts along other side of heel flap, then knit across the first 8 (9, 9, 10, 11) heel sts from Needle 1 again—70 (80, 84, 94, 100) sts total; 22 (25, 26, 29, 31) sts each on Needle 1 and Needle 3; 26 (30, 32, 36, 38) instep sts on Needle 2. Rnd now begins at center back heel.

Rnd 2: On Needle 1, knit to last 3 sts, k2tog, k1; on Needle 2, knit across all instep sts; on Needle 3, k1, ssk, knit to end—2 gusset sts dec'd.

Rnd 3: Knit.

Rep Rnds 2 and 3 until 52 (60, 64, 72, 76) sts rem—13 (15, 16, 18, 19) sts each on Needle 1 and Needle 3; 26 (30, 32, 36, 38) instep sts on Needle 2.

Foot

Work even until piece measures 5½ (6½, 7½, 8, 8¾)" (14 [16.5, 19, 20.5, 22] cm) from back of heel, or about 1½ (1¾, 2, 2¼, 2¼)" (3.8 [4.5, 5, 5.5, 5.5] cm) less than desired total foot length.

Toe

Rnd 1: On Needle 1, knit to last 3 sts, k2tog, k1; on Needle 2, k1, ssk, knit to last 3 sts, k2tog, k1; on Needle 3, k1, ssk, knit to end—4 sts dec'd.

Rnd 2: Knit.

Rep Rnds 1 and 2 until 24 (28, 32, 36, 40) sts rem. Rep Rnd 1 *only* until 8 (8, 12, 12, 16) sts rem. Knit sts from Needle 1 onto Needle 3—4 (4, 6, 6, 8) sts each on 2 needles.

Finishing

Cut yarn, leaving an 18" (45.5 cm) tail. Using the Kitchener st (see pages 42–45), graft sts tog. Weave in loose ends. Fold cuff to RS along fold line. Block.

Knee Socks

A lace pattern extends along the leg and instep of these knee-high socks. To accommodate the shape of the calf, extra stitches are cast on at the top of the leg (and worked with larger needles). Initially, there are 2 purl stitches between each lace pattern repeat, but along the length of the leg, each pair of purl stitches is decreased to 1 purl stitch, then that stitch is decreased away completely. Although the purl stitches are used solely for shaping, they add elasticity without disrupting the lace pattern. The cuff is worked in a knit 3, purl 2 rib that flows seamlessly into the lace pattern.

The instructions here are modified from the basic sock pattern for 7 stitches to the inch (see page 54) worked on four double-pointed needles.

Finished Size

About 6½ (7½, 8, 9, 9¾)" (16.5 [19, 20.5, 23, 25] cm) foot circumference, about 7 (8¼, 9½, 10¼, 11)" (18 [21, 24, 26, 28] cm) foot length from back of heel to tip of toe, and about 10 (11½, 14¾, 14¾, 18)" (25.5 [29, 37.5, 37.5, 45.5] cm) leg length from upper edge to beginning of heel flap. To fit child medium (child large, adult small, adult medium, adult large); see page 51 for shoe size conversions. Socks shown measure 8" (20.5 cm) foot circumference.

Yarn

Sportweight (#2 Fine; see page 12).
Shown here: Louet Gems Sport Weight (100% wool; 225 yd [206 m]/100 g): willow, 2 (2, 2, 3, 3) skeins.

Needles

Upper leg—size 4 (3.75 mm): set of 4 double-pointed (dpn). Lower leg and foot—size 3 (3.25 mm): set of 4 dpn. Adjust needle size if necessary to obtain the correct gauge.

Notions

Marker; tapestry needle.

Gauge

14 stitches and 18 rounds = 2" (5 cm) in stockinette worked in the rnd on smaller needles; 48 rounds of zigzag lacy rib = 5" (12.5 cm) high worked in the round on larger needles.

Stitch Guide

Zigzag Lacy Rib (begins as multiple of 10 sts, decreases to multiple of 8 sts)

Rnd 1: *Yo, k3, ssk (see Glossary, page 133), k3, p2; rep from *.
Even-numbered Rnds 2–14: Knit the knits and purl the purls.
Rnd 3: *K1, yo, k3, ssk, k2, p2; rep from *.
Rnd 5: *K2, yo, k3, ssk, k1, p2; rep from *.
Rnd 7: *K3, yo, k3, ssk, p2; rep from *.

Rnd 9: *K3, k2tog, k3, yo, p2; rep from *.
Rnd 11: *K2, k2tog, k3, yo, k1, p2; rep from *.
Rnd 13: *K1, k2tog, k3, yo, k2, p2; rep from *.
Rnd 15: *K2tog, k3, yo, k3, p2; rep from *.
Rnd 16: Knit the knits and purl the purls, unless instructed to work this rnd as a dec rnd in the directions. After decreasing, patt continues as a multiple of 9 sts.
Rnd 17: *Yo, k3, ssk, k3, p1; rep from *.
Even-numbered Rnds 18–30: Knit the knits and purl the purls.
Rnd 19: *K1, yo, k3, ssk, k2, p1; rep from *.
Rnd 21: *K2, yo, k3, ssk, k1, p1; rep from *.
Rnd 23: *K3, yo, k3, ssk, p1; rep from *.
Rnd 25: *K3, k2tog, k3, yo, p1; rep from *.
Rnd 27: *K2, k2tog, k3, yo, k1, p1; rep from *.
Rnd 29: *K1, k2tog, k3, yo, k2, p1; rep from *.
Rnd 31: *K2tog, k3, yo, k3, p1; rep from *.
Rnd 32: Knit the knits and purl the purls, unless instructed to work this rnd as a dec rnd in the directions. After decreasing, patt continues as a multiple of 8 sts.
Rnd 33: *Yo, k3, ssk, k3; rep from *.
Even-numbered Rnds 34–46: Knit.
Rnd 35: *K1, yo, k3, ssk, k2; rep from *.
Rnd 37: *K2, yo, k3, ssk, k1; rep from *.
Rnd 39: *K3, yo, k3, ssk; rep from *.
Rnd 41: *K3, k2tog, k3, yo; rep from *.
Rnd 43: *K2, k2tog, k3, yo, k1; rep from *.
Rnd 45: *K1, k2tog, k3, yo, k2; rep from *.
Rnd 47: *K2tog, k3, yo, k3; rep from *.
Rnd 48: Knit.

Note

Be careful that you do not accidentally drop any yarnovers that occur at the end of a needle or the end of the round.

Leg

With larger needles, CO 60 (60, 70, 80, 90) sts. Place marker and join for working in rnds, being careful not to twist sts. Working k3, p2 rib until leg measures 1¾" (4.5 cm) from CO. Change to zigzag lacy rib patt (see Stitch Guide), and work as given for your size as foll:

Foot circumferences 6½" and 7½": Work 15 rnds in patt, ending with Rnd 15.

Foot circumferences 8" and 9": Work Rnds 1–16 once without decreasing on Rnd 16, then work Rnds 1–15 once more.

Foot circumference 9¾": Work Rnds 1–16 twice without decreasing on Rnd 16, then work Rnds 1–15 once more.

All sizes: Work Rnd 16 as a dec rnd as foll: *K8, p2tog; rep from *—54 (54, 63, 72, 81) sts rem; patt is a multiple of 9 sts; piece measures about 3½ (3½, 5, 5, 6¾)" (9 [9, 12.5, 12.5, 17] cm) from CO. Cont for your size as foll:

Foot circumferences 6½" and 7½": Work Rnds 17–31 of patt, ending 1 st before end of rnd on Rnd 31.

Foot circumferences 8" and 9": Work Rnds 17–32 once without decreasing on Rnd 32, then work Rnds 17–31 once more ending 1 st before end of rnd on Rnd 31.

Foot circumference 9¾": Work Rnds 17–32 twice without decreasing on Rnd 32, then work Rnds 17–31 once more ending 1 st before end of rnd on Rnd 31.

All sizes: Work Rnd 32 of patt as a dec rnd as foll: Sl unworked st at end of Rnd 31 to left-hand needle, k2tog (last st of Rnd 31 tog with first st of Rnd 32), *k7, k2tog; rep from * to last 7 sts, end k7—48 (48, 56, 64, 72) sts; patt is a multiple of 8 sts; piece measures about 5 (5, 8½, 8½, 11¾)" (12.5 [12.5, 21.5, 21.5, 30] cm) from CO. Rep Rnds 33–48 of patt 2 times— piece measures 8½ (8½, 11¾, 11¾, 15)" (21.5 [21.5, 30, 30, 38] cm) from CO. Change to smaller needles.

Foot circumference 6½": Work Rnds 33–47 of patt.

All other sizes: Work Rnds 33–48 of patt once, then work Rnds 33–47 once more—piece measures 10 (11½, 14¾, 14¾, 18)" (25.5 [29, 37.5, 37.5, 45.5] cm) from CO.

Heel

K16 (16, 14, 16, 22), turn work around and with same needle, purl the next 24 (24, 28, 32, 36) sts and dec 2 (inc 2, dec 0, dec 0, dec 2) sts evenly spaced as you go—22 (26, 28, 32, 34) heel sts on one needle. Place rem 24 (24, 28, 32, 36) sts on spare needle(s) or holder to work later for instep; the center 24 (24, 24, 32, 36) sts on instep needle are 3 (3, 3, 4, 4) complete patt reps with 0 (0, 2, 0, 2) sts in St st at each end of needle.

Heel Flap

Work back and forth on heel sts in rows as foll:

Row 1: (RS) *Sl 1 pwise with yarn in back (wyb), k1; rep from *.

Row 2: Sl 1 pwise with yarn in front (wyf), purl to end.

Rep Rows 1 and 2 until a total of 22 (26, 28, 32, 34) rows have been worked—11 (13, 14, 16, 17) chain selvedge sts.

Turn Heel

Work short-rows as foll:

Row 1: (RS) K13 (15, 16, 18, 19), ssk, k1, turn work.

Row 2: (WS) Sl 1 pwise, p5, p2tog, p1, turn.

Row 3: Sl 1 pwise, knit to 1 st before gap made on previous row, ssk (1 st from each side of gap), k1, turn.

Row 4: Sl 1 pwise, purl to 1 st before gap made on previous row, p2tog (1 st from each side of gap), p1, turn.

Repeat Rows 3 and 4 until all heel sts have been worked, ending with a WS row and ending the last repeat ssk on Row 3 and p2tog on Row 4 if there are not enough sts to work the final k1 or p1 after the dec—14 (16, 16, 18, 20) sts rem.

Gusset

Note: One extra st is picked up along the selvedge in the corner of each heel flap to avoid leaving a hole at the base of the gusset. Rejoin for working in the rnd as foll:

Rnd 1: With one needle (Needle 1), knit across all heel sts, then pick up and knit 12 (14, 15, 17, 18) sts along selvedge edge of heel flap; with another dpn (Needle 2), work instep sts as k0 (0, 2, 0, 2), work Row 48 of patt across next 24 (24, 24, 32, 32) sts, k0 (0, 2, 0, 2); with another dpn (Needle 3), pick up and knit 12 (14, 15, 17, 18) sts along other side of heel flap, then knit across the first 7 (8, 8, 9, 10) heel sts from Needle 1 again—62 (68, 74, 84, 92) sts total; 19 (22, 23, 26, 28) sts each on Needle 1 and Needle 3; 24 (24, 28, 32, 36) instep sts on Needle 2. Rnd now begins at center back heel; rep Rows 33–48 of patt on instep sts to end of foot.

Rnd 2: On Needle 1, knit to last 3 sts, k2tog, k1; on Needle 2, work instep sts in patt as established; on Needle 3, k1, ssk, knit to end—2 gusset sts dec'd.

Rnd 3: Knit.

Rep Rnds 2 and 3 until 44 (52, 56, 64, 68) sts rem—10 (14, 14, 16, 16) sts each on Needle 1 and Needle 3; 24 (24, 28, 32, 36) instep sts on Needle 2.

Foot

Cont as established, working instep sts in patt, until piece measures 5½ (6½, 7½, 8, 8¾)" (14 [16.5, 19, 20.5, 22] cm) from back of heel, or about 1½ (1¾, 2, 2¼, 2¼)" (3.8 [4.5, 5, 5.5, 5.5] cm) less than desired total foot length, ending with Rnd 39, 40, 47, or 48 of patt.

Toe

Rearrange sts so there are 11 (13, 14, 16, 17) sts each on Needle 1 and Needle 3 and 22 (26, 28, 32, 34) sts on Needle 2. Work all sts in St st as foll:

Rnd 1: On Needle 1, knit to last 3 sts, k2tog, k1; on Needle 2, k1, ssk, work to last 3 sts, k2tog, k1; on Needle 3, k1, ssk, knit to end— 4 sts dec'd.

Rnd 2: Knit.

Rep Rnds 1 and 2 until 20 (24, 28, 32, 36) sts rem. Rep Rnd 1 *only* until 8 (8, 8, 12, 12) sts rem. Knit sts from Needle 1 onto Needle 3—4 (4, 4, 6, 6) sts each on 2 needles.

Finishing

Cut yarn, leaving an 18" (45.5 cm) tail. Using the Kitchener st (see pages 42–45), graft sts tog.

Glossary of Abbreviations and Terms

ABBREVIATIONS

beg	begin(s); beginning
BO	bind off
CC	contrast color
cm	centimeter(s)
cn	cable needle
CO	cast on
dec(s)	decrease(s); decreasing
dpn	double-pointed needles
foll	follow(s); following
g	gram(s)
inc(s)	increase(s); increasing
k	knit
k1f&b	knit into the front and back of same st
kwise	knitwise, as if to knit
m	marker(s)
MC	main color
mm	millimeter(s)
M1	make one (increase)
p	purl
p1f&b	purl into front and back of same st
patt(s)	pattern(s)
psso	pass slipped st over
pwise	purlwise, as if to purl
rem	remain(s); remaining
rep	repeat(s)
rev St st	reverse stockinette stitch
rnd(s)	round(s)
RS	right side
sl	slip
sl st	slip st (slip 1 st pwise unless otherwise indicated)
ssk	slip 2 sts kwise, one at a time, from the left needle to right needle, insert left needle tip through both front loops and knit together from this position (1 st decrease)
St st	stockinette stitch
tbl	through back loop
tog	together
WS	wrong side
wyb	with yarn in back
wyf	with yarn in front
yd	yard(s)
yo	yarn over
*	repeat starting point
* *	repeat all instructions between asterisks
( )	alternate measurements and/or instructions
[ ]	work instructions as a group a specified number of times

Decreases

K2tog

Knit 2 stitches together as if they were a single stitch   2 stitches are reduced to 1.

P2tog

Purl 2 stitches together as if they were a single stitch—2 stitches are reduced to 1.

Ssk

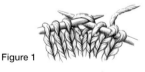

Figure 1

Figure 2

Slip 2 stitches individually knitwise (Figure 1), insert left needle tip into the front of these 2 slipped stitches, and use the right needle to knit them together through their back loops (Figure 2)—2 stitches are reduced to 1.

Increases

K1f&b

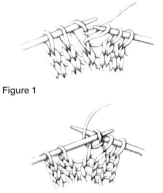

Figure 1

Figure 2

Knit into a stitch but leave it on the left needle (Figure 1), then knit through the back loop of the same stitch (Figure 2) and slip the original stitch off the needle.

Yo

Wrap the working yarn around the needle from front to back, then bring yarn into position to work the next stitch (leave it in back if a knit stitch follows; bring it under the needle to the front if a purl stitch follows).

Duplicate Stitch

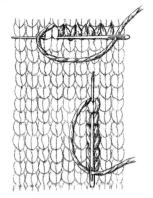

Horizontal: Bring threaded needle out from back to front at the base of the V of the knitted stitch you want to cover. *Working right to left, pass the needle in and out under the stitch in the row above it and back into the base of the same stitch. Bring the needle back out at the base of the V and the next stitch to the left. Repeat from * for each stitch to be covered.

Vertical: Beginning at lowest point, work as for horizontal duplicate stitch, ending by bringing the needle back out at the base of the stitch directly above the stitch just worked.

Sources for Supplies

Brown Sheep Company
100662 Cty. Rd. 16
Mitchell, NE 69357
(308) 635-2198
www.brownsheep.com
> **Nature Spun Sport** (sportweight wool yarn available in dozens of colors)
> **Lamb's Pride Superwash Worsted** (worsted-weight wool yarn that's machine washable)

Cascade Yarns
PO Box 58168
1224 Andover Park East
Tukwila, WA 98188
(206) 574-0440
www.cascadeyarns.com
> **Fixation** (sportweight cotton/elastic yarn that has lots of stretch)

Coats & Clark
8 Shelter Dr.
Greer, SC 29650
www.coatsandclark.com
> **TLC Amore Solid** (chunky-weight acrylic yarn that's delightfully soft)

Koigu Wool Designs
RR #1 Williamsford, ON
Canada N0H 2V0
(519) 794-3066, (888) 765-WOOL
www.koigu.com
> **Koigu Premium Merino** (super-soft fingering-weight wool yarn in beautiful handdyed colors)

Lana Grossa
Distributed in the United States and Canada by Unicorn Books & Crafts Inc.
1338 Ross St.
Petaluma, CA 94954
(707) 762-3362, (800) 289-9276
www.lanagrossa.com
> **Meilenweit Cotton Fun & Stripes** (fingering-weight cotton/wool/polyamide yarn in self-striping colors)

Lion Brand Yarns
135 Kero Rd.
Carlstadt, NJ 07072
(800) 258-9276
www.lionbrand.com
> **Magic Stripes** (fingering-weight superwash wool/nylon yarn that creates its own Fair Isle pattern)
> **Wool Prints** (worsted-weight wool yarn in self-patterning colors)

Lorna's Laces
4229 N. Honore St.
Chicago, IL 60613
(773) 935-3803
www.lornaslaces.net
> **Shepherd Sock** (fingering-weight superwash wool/nylon yarn in beautiful handdyed colors)

Louet North America
808 Commerce Park Dr.
Odgensburg, NY 13669
(613) 925-4502, (800) 897-6444
www.louet.com
> **Gems Fingering Weight** (fingering-weight superwash wool yarn in beautiful colors)
> **Gems Sport Weight** (sportweight superwash wool yarn)
> **Gems Worsted Weight** (worsted-weight superwash wool yarn)
> **Gems Chunky Weight** (chunky-weight superwash wool yarn)

The Wooly West
PO Box 58306
Salt Lake City, UT 84158
(801) 581-9812
www.woolywest.com
> **Footpath** (fingering-weight wool/nylon yarn in heathered colors)

Westminster Fibers
4 Townsend West, Unit 8
Nashua, NH 03063
www.westminsterfibers.com
> **Regia 4-Ply Stretch Crazy Color** (fingering-weight wool/polyamide yarn in self-striping colors)

For more knitting designs and techniques, join the community at knittingdaily.com, where life meets knitting, or subscribe to Interweave's knitting magazines:
Interweave Crochet, Interweave Knits, Knitscene, PieceWork, Spin-Off

Bibliography

Bordhi, Cat. *Socks Soar on Two Circular Needles: A Manual of Elegant Knitting Techniques and Patterns.* Friday Harbor, Washington: Passing Paws Press, 2001.

Budd, Ann. *The Knitter's Handy Book of Patterns: Basic Designs in Multiple Sizes & Gauges.* Loveland, Colorado: Interweave Press, 2002.

Budd, Ann and Anne Merrow, editors. *Favorite Socks: 25 Timeless Designs from Interweave.* Loveland, Colorado: Interweave Press, 2006.

Bush, Nancy. *Folk Knitting in Estonia.* Loveland, Colorado: Interweave Press, 1999.

Bush, Nancy. *Folk Socks: The History & Techniques of Handknitted Footwear.* Loveland, Colorado: Interweave Press, 1994.

Bush, Nancy. *Knitting Vintage Socks: New Twists on Classic Patterns.* Loveland, Colorado: Interweave Press, 2005.

Galeskas, Bev. *The Magic Loop: Working Around on One Needle.* East Wenatchee, Washington: Fiber Trends, 2002.

Gibson-Roberts, Priscilla. *Simple Socks Plain and Fancy.* Cedaredge, Colorado: Nomad Press, 2001.

Knight, Erika, editor. *Harmony Guide: Cables and Arans.* Loveland, Colorado: Interweave Press, 2007.

——. *Harmony Guide: Knitting and Purl.* Loveland, Colorado: Interweave Press, 2007

——. *Harmony Guide: Lace and Eyelets.* Loveland, Colorado: Interweave Press, 2007

Schurch, Charlene. *Sensational Knitted Socks.* Woodinville, Washington: Martingale and Company, 2005.

Walker, Barbara G. *A Treasury of Knitting Patterns* and *A Second Treasury of Knitting Patterns* Pittsville, Wisconsin: Schoolhouse Press, 1998.

Index

basics, sock 15–16; instructions 49–61
bibliography 135
bind-offs 45
blocking 46
bouclé socks 72–73

cable patterns 96–107
casting on 22
cast-ons 20–22
clocks 96, 104–107
Continental cast-on 20
color 10, 62–73
color, adding 74–83
cuffs 24
cuff variations 120–121; picot 122–124; ruffle 125–127

darning 38
decreases 133
duplicate stitch 133

ends, weaving in loose 45

fiber content 10
fit, improper 38; proper 36
finishing 45
flexible cast-on 20, 22
foot 37

gathered toe tip 45
gauge 9, 12, 17, 74
glossary 132–133
grafting 42–44
gussets 30–36; close holes in 46; decrease stitches at 34–36; pick up and knit along 30; prevent holes at 31

heel flap 26; stitches 27
heel turn 28–29
holes, preventing 38

increases 133

join to work in round 23
joins, crossover 23; simple 23

Kitchener stitch 42–44
knee socks 128–131
knit one front and back (k1f&b) 133
knit two together (k2tog) 133

lace patterns 108–111
legs 25; fitting 36
lengths, matching 27
long-tail cast-on 20

measurements for fit, foot 37, 49; leg 36, 49; sock 15–16, 49–51

needles 11–12
needles, knitting with circular 18–19; double-pointed 18

Old Norwegian cast-on 21

patterns, cable 96–107; cable clock 104–107; chevron lace 116–119; herringbone lace 112–115; lace 108–119; rib 84–87; right-twist cable rib 100–103; seeded rib 88–91; spiral rib 92–95; texture 74–75;
pick up and knit along gussets 30
purl two together (p2tog) 133

reinforcing yarn 38
rib patterns 84–87
rounds, knitting 18–19, 23–24

short-rows 28–29
size chart 51
size, choosing 49–51
slip slip knit (ssk) 133
sources 134
splicing yarns 83
stitches, loose 25
stripe patterns 75
stripes, Fibonacci 76–79; magic 70–71; magic ball 80–83; narrow 66–67; spiral 68–69; wide 64–65

three-needle bind-off 45
toe 39–41
tools 13
two-end join 23

wedge toe 39
wet-splice yarns 83

yarn 9–10
yarn colors 63
yarn, chunky-weight 60; DK-weight 56–57; fingering-weight 52–55; sportweight 54–57; worsted-weight 58–59
yarnover 133
yarn, self-patterning 63
yarn standards 12
yarn weight 9, instructions for different 52–61